PAID IN FULL

40-Day Healing Ministry
ACTIVATION MANUAL

A 40-Day Journey of Practical
Activation in Healing Ministry

Art Thomas
James Loruss
Jonathan Ammon

LEGAL DISCLAIMER: This book and the accompanying movie, *Paid in Full*, are about the Christian practice of "divine healing" and are not to be construed as instruction or advice concerning medicine or medical treatment. No portion of this text or the film is presented as a substitute for medical care. The terms "train," "teach," and/or "equip" (and any similar terms) are to be understood in the context of religious practice and not medical science. Any discussion of "methods" or "actions" on the part of the authors or people who have participated in the film are not to be construed as medical training or counsel and are strictly to be perceived as a religious study and investigation of a Biblical topic.

Acknowledgements:

Art Thomas:

I'd like to thank my wife, Robin, for supporting me in ministry and for enabling me to devote so much time to this book and its accompanying film; my parents, for their lifelong support, encouragement, and Christian examples; my pastor, Brooks McElhenny, for his friendship and support of my ministry; and Jesus, for paying the price to make the topic of this book a reality worth studying, embracing, and practicing no matter the cost.

James Loruss:

I'd like to thank my parents for supporting me every step of the way in my ministry; my father for setting an example of how Jesus would lead a home; my mother for teaching me the heart of a servant; my pastor, Brooks McElhenny, and his family for being a second family to me and supporting me as a minister of the Gospel. I'd also like to thank my future wife for being awesome, because I know you will be!

Jonathan Ammon:

I would like to acknowledge the Lord Jesus Christ who loved us so much that He took our sin, pain, and sickness; my parents who have been the voice of healing and unconditional love in my life and who introduced me to The Healer and His miracles again and again; and Art Thomas who has taught me more about divine healing than anyone.

Table of Contents

Introduction

Chances are, you're reading this book after having watched our movie, *Paid in Full: God's Desire to Heal through Today's Believers.* And chances are, if you just watched that movie, you're still processing much of what you saw and heard.

God's healing power truly is amazing, and what He's doing around the world can be stunning and mind-blowing—especially when you realize that you've been invited to do the same exact things! This daily training manual is designed to help you apply the message of the movie to your own life and ministry.

Our goal in presenting this material to you is to see the entire Body of Christ being just as effective at ministering healing as the literal, physical body of Christ was when He walked this earth.

> **Luke 6:19**—And the whole multitude sought to touch Him, for power went out from Him and healed them all. (NKJV)

In Acts 5:12, we see that all the believers were meeting together in Solomon's Colonnade. In verse 16, we learn that every single sick or demonized person who came to them was completely healed.

We believe that healing ministry — like evangelism — is the responsibility of the entire Body of Christ. The three of us developed this training manual believing that 100% results are possible — not because every person we personally pray for is healed, but because we have each been in multiple meetings where every person was healed as the Body of Christ in that place ministered together. More importantly, 100% results are found both in the life of Jesus and — at times — in the early church. (We'll support these claims through our study.)

Again, like evangelism, healing ministry is all of our responsibility. Every time someone dies in their sin, the Church needs to do a collective self-assessment, asking, "Could we have been more effective at presenting Jesus and His Gospel?" But as an individual, I must also ask, "What is my role in becoming more effective at evangelism?"

It's not that I am directly responsible for a person dying without receiving salvation. Anyone from the Body of Christ could have reached them with the Gospel — yet none of us did — so all of us need to change. But the fact remains that I must examine my own effectiveness if the entire Church is ever going to grow.

The same goes for healing ministry. People are not being healed, and the responsibility lies on the entire Church. No individual is at fault when the sick are not healed. Nevertheless, I must still examine my own effectiveness and seek to grow so that we can see Jesus receive everything for which He paid.

This is why we made the movie, *Paid in Full,* and this is why we wrote this book. Our desire is to see healing ministry restored as a normal function of the entire Body of Christ—not merely one congregation here or one minister there but the *entire* Church.

Jesus gave "some" to train and equip the Church—the ultimate goal being that every one of us would attain to "the whole measure of the fullness of Christ" (Ephesians 4:11-13). The "some" who Jesus gave to the Church are not the ministers; the people of the Church are the ministers. The "some" are the "equippers" who devote their hearts and lives to helping every Christian look just like Jesus in nature, character, mission, love, and ministry. This is our passion, and this targeted manual is designed to help each reader look more like Jesus specifically in regard to healing ministry. As we—the Body of Christ—grow together, we expect to see a more complete expression of Jesus throughout the world. We will all learn from each other, the sick will be healed, and souls will be saved.

We wrote each lesson to help you take personal responsibility for your own role in healing ministry. You will be challenged to think, feel, and act. Your theology may be stretched as you're encouraged to think in different ways than you have previously been taught. In all things, test what we have to say and see if it stands the tests of Scripture, sound reason, and the nature and example of Jesus Christ.

We speak with certainty and passion because we have tried and tested our views through experience, but we still recognize our fallibility and the possibility of being wrong. Feel free to disagree with or question anything you read. Write your questions in the margins. Debate your thoughts with trusted Christian friends (especially those who are seeing more results than you). See if there is any Scripture to support your disagreement. You may learn more from wrestling with this text than from the text itself!

In each lesson, you will find a quote from one of the people in our movie—either from the film itself or from extra footage we have of that person. We'll share a short scripture passage with you and a lesson on the given topic. Then you'll be encouraged to pray about the topic, journal briefly, and look for an opportunity to act on what you've learned. Supplemental Scripture reading is also listed at the end of each lesson for those who want to dig a little deeper into the given topic.

In just a few minutes each day, you can discover the same Biblical insights and practical principles that moved all three of us from seeing zero results in healing ministry to now seeing a majority of people healed in Jesus' name. And when your 40-day study is complete, we're believing that you will have already ministered healing to more people than you can count.

Do I Need to Watch the Movie
Paid in Full to Benefit from this Book?

We purposely designed this book to stand alone as a powerful tool to help launch people into healing ministry. If you've never seen our movie,

Paid in Full, that's perfectly alright! This book will still offer you a complete training in healing ministry.

With that said, the documentary we made has been an eye-opener for many people, and no book can accomplish what happens when you actually witness miracles happening. If there is a reasonable way for you to see our film about God's desire to heal through you, we highly recommend it. The full movie can be ordered at www.PaidInFullFilm.com.

Ways to Use this Book

There are two recommended ways for using this book:

First, you may choose to go through this training as a matter of personal devotional study and enrichment. In this case, the best way to read it is to first watch the film and then read one lesson per day for the next 40 days. There's nothing wrong with starting the study before watching the film, but seeing the movie is perhaps the best way to get your feet wet regarding this topic.

Second, while this book stands alone as its own text, it is also designed to serve as supplemental reading that accompanies an 8-week *Paid in Full* DVD Small Group Study, which can be purchased at www.PaidInFullFilm.com. In order to make the lessons in this book line up with the small group curriculum, begin reading "Day 1" after the first small group meeting (where you will watch the documentary, *Paid in Full,* together); and then only read one section (five lessons) per week. The lessons you study that week will help fuel discussion at your next meeting because you will have been thinking about and acting on that topic for several days already. Then, after your final small group session on the eighth week, this book will continue with one more section about "Maturing in the Ministry of Healing," which will help you to keep walking in what you've learned.

We recommend reading in the morning because of the "Action Step" at the end of each lesson, which should be accomplished somehow that day. If you prefer to read at night, be sure to look again at the "Action Step" the next morning so that it's fresh in your mind throughout the day. The Action Steps are perhaps the most important parts because we generally learn much more through experience than through mere reading. Be sure to journal about your experiences for the sake of personal memory and declaring the wonders of God.

If you ever find yourself missing an Action Step, you can do one of two things: (1) Wait to read the next lesson until you fulfill the challenge presented in the Action Step, or (2) Somehow mark that page of the book and return to it after you have completed the entire study.

Are You Ready?

Paid in Full is more than a film; it's an experience. The same is true of this book! In your hands is an invitation to discover new insights about God's desire to heal through you. More than that, it is a vehicle for moving you along in His plan and growing your faith in Him and expectation for physical healing.

All three of us have witnessed well over one

thousand miraculous healings in the last year alone. We've seen everything from blind eyes and deaf ears opening to tumors and hernia disappearing to blood-sugar and blood-pressure regulating. And our experience has been that absolutely any Christian of any age (even children) can minister healing with just as much authority, power, and effectiveness as the people we look up to in the Bible.

In fact, of the three of us, not one of us was seeing any healings as recently as five years ago. The Lord produced quick results in our lives, and we believe He will do the same for you. Nevertheless, this didn't come without many trials, emotional hardships, relational mistakes, and various sacrifices. As Joe Funaro said in our film, "The healing ministry is not some glorified ministry. And to be honest with you, there is hardship, and you've got to prepare yourself for that. And you've got to establish yourself in the fact that this is God's will, and that this is something you're going to do, and that you're going to be totally dependent on God because there are hardships in this ministry and there are difficult times. You have to prepare yourself for that, or just know that it's going to come; and just dig your feet in, stay at it, and don't quit, because you know it's the will of God."

Our prayer for you is that you will rise above every hardship and persevere so that you will see many people physically healed. But more importantly, we pray that you will see many come to salvation as the Lord works with you, confirming His word by the signs that accompany it. (See Mark 16:20.) Healing ministry is a valuable ministry, and God is ready to use you!

It doesn't really matter which day of the week

you start reading this study, but there's no time like the present, so lets dig in!

SECTION 1:
Is Healing *Really* for Everyone?

Day 1
Does God Want to Minister Healing through All Christians or Only a Few?

Art Thomas

What Jesus modeled was this ministry of preaching, teaching, and healing. And I think that healing ministry should be a part of every ministry. I don't think there should be any ministry where healing is not part and parcel with the work that God is doing because it's His desire to heal.

~ Daniel Kolenda

> **Mark 16:17-18** — And these signs will follow those who believe: In My name they will cast out demons; they will speak with new tongues; they will take up serpents; and if they drink anything deadly, it will by no means hurt them; they will lay hands on the sick, and they will recover. (NKJV)

The promises of Mark 16 are not for a select few

believers — they're for every believer. "Casting out demons" is not a gift of the Spirit — it's something every Christian has the authority to do in Jesus' name. On the day of Pentecost, "all of them...began to speak in other tongues as the Spirit enabled them" (Acts 2:1-4). And God's supernatural protection (whether from dangerous animals or deadly poison) is not a gift for a few, but rather a sign that has been promised to those who preach the Gospel in Jesus' name. Similarly, the promise that we will lay our hands on the sick and see them recover is for all believers.

Mark 16 is the passage that drove me into healing ministry. I heard another minister — Todd White — say, "Jesus said these signs will accompany those who believe. So if these signs don't accompany you, then there must be something up with your belief!" Todd's words angered and frustrated me. I was a youth pastor who had credentials with a major Pentecostal denomination. We believe firmly in God's power to heal! And yet I had prayed for hundreds of people without seeing results.

I had to face reality: Todd was talking about me.

I committed myself to study what the Word of God says about healing, and for the next three months, that's all I studied. I brought every one of my questions to the Lord — every argument and every scripture that I thought would prove Todd wrong. Instead, I found Jesus kept proving him right.

As soon as I decided to agree that God always wanted to heal and that He always wanted to use me to do it, I began to see results. It took me three months to reach that conclusion; but once it was settled, there was no turning back. Prior to that decision in August 2009, I could count the number of miracles I had witnessed on two hands—and none of them happened through my own prayers. Since then, however, I've watched Jesus perform thousands of miracles—not only through my hands but through hundreds of men, women, and children from around the world.

As you walk through this study with me and my two partners in ministry, I am expecting the same results for you. These signs WILL follow you if you will simply believe Jesus. He wants to heal the sick through you!

Prayer Starter:

- ❏ Take a moment to thank the Lord for His invitation to partner with Him in ministering healing to the sick.
- ❏ Ask the Holy Spirit to give you wisdom and discernment as you study the topic of healing ministry, and ask Him to open the eyes of your heart to His truth.
- ❏ Ask God for fresh opportunities to pray for the sick with the measure of faith He knows you have.

Journal Experience:

What are your biggest questions about God's desire to heal the sick through you? Specifically, write down the most faith-consuming arguments against this being true that you find holding you back from jumping wholeheartedly into healing ministry.

_____

_____

_____

_____

_____

_____

_____

_____

_____

_____

_____

_____

_____

_____

_____

_____

_____

Action Step:

God's intent for healing ministry is that it would confirm the message of the Gospel: that Jesus has the power to save, and that His blood is still effective today. One of the easiest ways to preach the Gospel is to share your own personal testimony of transformation.

Your personal testimony has three parts: (1) What your life used to look like, (2) the event(s) that God used to draw you to Himself, and (3) how His work in you had affected your life since then.

If you don't have a testimony, then you need to get saved! Surrender your life to Jesus today. This book will not be of any value to you unless you are serving and loving Him with your whole heart, soul, mind, and strength. Simply admit verbally that Jesus is indeed Lord—that He is deserving of your entire life and that He truly has all authority in heaven and on earth. Second, choose to believe wholeheartedly that God raised Him from the dead—which means He is alive today, and that same resurrection power is available to transform you into a new creation.

Now, consider the three parts of your testimony, and find someone with whom to share it. If you're nervous, share it with another Christian to practice, but I would encourage you to share with someone you know (or even a complete stranger) who you don't think knows Jesus.

Supplemental Reading:
- Matthew 10:7-8
- Luke 10:1 and 9
- John 14:12
- Acts 5:12 and 16

DAY 2
IS IT ALWAYS GOD'S WILL TO HEAL?

Art Thomas

Well, if you consider scripture, Jesus Christ is perfect theology. He modeled and demonstrated the heart of the Father in every situation. And if you read through the entire New Testament — especially the Gospels — you'll see that He never turned anyone away. He never told anyone that "you'll have to wait — God's trying to teach you something." He did just the opposite. He healed everyone who came to Him.

~ Les Coombs

> **Hebrews 1:3a** — The Son is the radiance of God's glory and the exact representation of His being, sustaining all things by His powerful word... (NIV)

Second Peter 3:9 tells us that God doesn't want anyone to perish but wants all to come to repentance; and yet we know from other scriptures that there are people who do indeed perish in their sin. Think about that: God's will is that no one perish, and yet people perish.

Some people ask, "If it's always God's will to heal people, then why isn't everyone healed? To them I ask, "If it's God's will for no one to perish, why do people perish?"

There is a human component at play. In Jesus' ministry, every single person who came to Him, who called out to Him, or who had someone else come on their behalf was healed. There are nine different passages that specifically say Jesus healed all (Matthew 4:24; 8:16; 9:35; 12:15; 14:35-36; Mark 6:56; Luke 4:40; 6:18b-19; and Acts 10:38).

This raises some heavy emotional issues that we'll address in greater measure later in our study — perhaps the greatest is this: Did my loved one die because I did something wrong?

Suppose I come to you and say that my dear, sweet Grandmother — whom everybody loved — died without coming to know Jesus, and then I ask you where she is now. You would hopefully be careful and tactful in your response; but ultimately — if you hold to orthodox theology — you're going to have to land on the point that she's not in heaven. Naturally, if no one helps me process this information, I'm going to be put into an emotional tailspin wondering if I could have done a better job presenting Jesus to her. What if I had loved her more or articulated the Gospel better? God didn't want her to perish, Jesus commissioned me to preach the Gospel, and yet my Grandma died in her sin.

Christianity is full of difficult truths that trouble our emotions. But truth doesn't exist to keep us happy. Truth often spurs us toward something higher than our current experience. People die in their sins while on our watch, and people also die of sickness and disease on our watch. In both cases, we need to leave the burden with Jesus and allow Him to help us grow to be more like Him so that we're even more effective next time.

More on that later. For now, know this: The fact that people are not healed does not disprove God's will to heal all. Rather than building our theology out of heartache, disappointment, or emotions, we need to build our theology on Jesus. He alone is "the exact representation of [the Father's] being," and He healed all.

Prayer Starter:

- ❏ Thank Jesus for perfectly representing the heart and will of the Father so that we wouldn't be left guessing about God's nature.
- ❏ If you've ever prayed for someone who wasn't healed, ask the Lord to take the emotional weight of that burden from you so that you can move forward in serving Him with joy.
- ❏ Ask the Lord for more people to cross your path who need physical healing so that you can practice and learn to see greater results.

Journal Experience:

Ask the Lord why He considers healing ministry to be important. Write down the thoughts that come to your mind that seem to answer that question.

_____

_____

_____

_____

_____

_____

_____

_____

_____

_____

_____

_____

_____

_____

_____

_____

_____

_____

_____

_____

Action Step:

Call, e-mail, or find someone who needs physical healing, and tell them, "I believe Jesus wants you to be healed." See where the conversation goes from there. If an opportunity arises for you to minister healing, do what you saw demonstrated when you watched the movie: simple prayers or commands, test it out, persevere. Allow the other person to "lead" by asking permission before doing or saying anything to minister, and check with them each time you're going to pray again. This shows love and respect for the person and allows them to exercise their own faith by deciding whether or not they want you to continue.

Supplemental Reading:
- ❑ Matthew 4:24
- ❑ Matthew 8:16
- ❑ Matthew 9:35
- ❑ Matthew 12:15;
- ❑ Matthew 14:35-36
- ❑ Mark 6:56
- ❑ Luke 4:40
- ❑ Luke 6:18b-19
- ❑ Acts 10:38

DAY 3
DOES GOD EVER MAKE PEOPLE SICK?

Art Thomas

You know, the mistake people make is that God is so good at turning bad stuff into something beautiful that people think that He sent it. That's not it. It's His goodness because He has the ability to take something that looks like trash, and turn it around, and make it beautiful.

~ Paul Manwaring

> **Luke 9:56** — For the Son of Man did not come to destroy men's lives but to save them." (NKJV)

After reading the opening quote and scripture passage, you may be surprised to see me say this: Yes, there are times when God makes people sick. The Old Testament is full of such examples. But those cases specifically had to do with a response to people breaking the Law, which Jesus cancelled for Christians so that it would no longer stand against us (Colossians 2:14).

In the New Testament, we only see one case where Jesus struck a person blind and only one case where a Christian cursed a person with blindness. The first case was Saul on the road to Damascus when Jesus appeared to him in a vision, and he was left blinded by the encounter (Acts 9:8-9). The second was a sorcerer named Bar-Jesus who opposed Barnabas and Saul and tried to turn a government official away from his newfound faith. Then Saul rebuked him and told him that he would be blind for a time (Acts 13:6-12).

In both cases, the person struck blind was an enemy of the Gospel. Saul was on his way to murder Christians, and Bar-Jesus was contradicting the message and persuading people away from it. So the only New Testament cases of God afflicting people with a problem (in both cases, blindness) happened to people who were active opponents of the Gospel of Jesus Christ. And in both cases, the condition was only temporary — Bar-Jesus was only blind "for a time" (Acts 13:11), and Saul was only blind for three days until a Christian came and ministered healing to him (Acts 9:10-19).

And that's an interesting point: In both cases, God's will was still healing! Even when God caused the condition, He still wanted to heal it. So anytime I encounter a sickness or disease, I don't worry about whether or not God caused the condition. Jesus never turned someone away saying, "Sorry, My Father did this one, so you're out of luck." He always healed. And Saul's blindness proves that the cause of the sickness is irrelevant when it comes to the fact that God desires to heal.

Romans 8:28 tells us that God works all situations together for the good of those who love

Him. This doesn't require God to have caused the problem we're facing; it simply means that He holds the solution.

Prayer Starter:

- ❑ Worship God for His awesomeness and allow a healthy fear of God to grip your heart—one that reminds you of His ability to destroy and yet His continual choice to love and give life.
- ❑ The ratio of people Jesus healed (hundreds and perhaps thousands) to people He afflicted with disease (only Saul) is staggering. Ask the Lord if there's anything in your heart that desires calamity for sinners more than healing, and then ask Him to change that in you so that your expectations line up more closely with His.
- ❑ Ask the Lord to lead you to someone who doesn't know Him but who He wants to heal physically. Pray for this person to be receptive when you come.

Journal Experience:

How would you explain to someone that God wants to heal them when they are convinced that He gave them their condition to produce holiness in their life or keep them humble?

_____

_____

_____

_____

_____

_____

_____

_____

_____

_____

_____

_____

_____

_____

_____

_____

_____

_____

Action Step:

During the prayer time, you asked God to lead you to someone who doesn't know Him but who He wants to heal physically. If you already know who that person is, give them a call or pay them a visit. If you don't know who the person is, keep your eyes open today, and be prepared to jump into action. Tell the person that God loves them and wants them to be healed. Admit that you're not perfect at representing Him, but that you'd like to please God by ministering healing to the person. Then ask if you can pray for them.

Supplemental Reading:
❏   Acts 9:1-19

DAY 4
IS THERE EVER A TIME WHEN GOD DOESN'T WANT TO HEAL?

Art Thomas

Every person that came to Jesus was healed. Not a single one did He leave untouched...by healing. And the reality is that it's His will to heal every time. So for me, I just take that expectation that wherever I go, I know — whether it's a bad headache or a broken bone — I know it's God's will to heal right now because He paid for it all.

~ *Steve Moore*

> **2 Corinthians 6:2b** — ...Behold, now is the accepted time; behold, now is the day of salvation (NKJV)

Our standard for everything we believe about healing ministry has to be Jesus Christ. Almost every person He healed was instantly healed. Only a few weren't instant, but even those happened within the same day. We never see Jesus saying, "My Father says, 'Not yet,' so you'll have to wait until the next time I pass through your village." He always healed, and it always happened that same day.

The Greek word for "salvation" can also be translated as "health." Similarly, the Greek word for "save" implies complete wholeness of body, soul, and spirit. Paul said that "now is the day of salvation." For me, this settles the matter. Jesus wants it now.

We like to teach people that sometimes God's answer to our prayer is "no" or "not yet." That's great advice in most cases — like, say, asking Him to provide a job opportunity, and He delays in answering because He knows the job opening in a couple weeks is much better for you. But when it comes to such things as forgiveness, healing, and deliverance from demons, the answer is always the same: "Now is the day of salvation." Your new job wasn't purchased with His blood. Your forgiveness, healing, and deliverance were.

NOW is the day of salvation! As stated in the film, truly believing this changes the way you minister. It moves you to persevere in ministry until you see results — each time holding the conviction that God actually wants this to happen right now.

Perhaps you know testimonies of people who received prayer and then experienced their healing days or weeks later. I do too! But I can't base my theology or expectation on that. Those testimonies did happen, and it was indeed God who performed the healing! But I have to base my theology and expectation on the example of Jesus; and He healed everyone within the day (and most of them immediately).

Prayer Starter:

- ❏ Thank the Lord for deciding 2000 years ago to pay the price for all forgiveness, healing, and deliverance.
- ❏ Ask Him to remove any doubt in your heart about Him wanting to heal immediately through you.
- ❏ Pray for God to give you immediate results when you minister healing to people.

Journal Experience:

Do you expect God to heal people immediately when you minister to them in Jesus' name? Why or why not?

_____

_____

_____

_____

_____

_____

_____

_____

_____

_____

_____

_____

_____

_____

_____

_____

_____

Action Step:

Ask the Lord to lead you to someone today who needs physical healing. When you find them, at some point tell them, "I believe God wants to heal you today." Then offer to pray for them.

Supplemental Reading:
- Matthew 8:3
- Matthew 20:34
- Mark 1:42
- Mark 5:29
- Mark 5:42
- Mark 10:52
- Luke 13:13

DAY 5
IS THERE ANYONE GOD WON'T USE
TO MINISTER HEALING?

Art Thomas

When we start understanding His grace – that we don't have to arrive at some level to start seeing his power move – that's when breakthrough happens... Up until that point, we keep comparing ourselves: "Am I good enough? Have I done it all right? Did I pray enough this week? Did I read my Bible enough? Did I do all the right things that I need to do to make this happen?" But it's not that. It's none of that. You know, God wants us to commune with Him and fellowship with Him, but His grace covers a multitude of wrongdoings, incorrect attitudes, or thoughts. God wants to do the work, even through imperfect people... And so, when we finally recognize His grace and His goodness, that'll be a breakthrough moment.
~ *Tim Gingrich*

Matthew 7:21-23 — Not everyone who says to Me, 'Lord, Lord,' shall enter the kingdom of heaven, but he who does the will of My Father in heaven. Many will say to Me in that day, 'Lord, Lord, have we not prophesied in Your name, cast out demons in Your name, and done many wonders in Your name?' And then I will declare to them, 'I never knew you; depart from Me, you who practice lawlessness!' (NKJV)

Jesus is incredibly passionate about the Gospel message being confirmed and demonstrated—so much so that He will use imperfect people to do it!

In Luke 9, Jesus sent out His twelve disciples to preach about the kingdom with power and authority over all kinds of sickness and disease, and they did it. But before that chapter even ends, these same "ministers" begin arguing over who is the greatest (verse 46), stopping others from ministering (verse 49), and even desiring to "call down fire" and murder an entire village of people who hadn't accepted them (verse 54). These men—who had just gone from village to village in Jesus' name to preach and heal—were prideful, exclusive, and even murderous.

Naturally, you would expect this to give Jesus pause about sending people in His name who weren't ready. But in the first verse of the very next chapter, He sends out seventy-two others! As if that isn't enough, when we reach Luke 11, one of the disciples asks, "Lord, teach us to pray" (verse 1). They weren't even confident in their prayer lives yet!

One's usefulness in healing ministry does not depend upon his or her relationship with Jesus, or level of integrity, or measure of holiness. After healing the man at the Temple gate, Peter proclaimed, "Why do you stare at us as if by our own power or godliness we had made this man walk?" (Acts 3:12). Your relationship with Jesus and God's ability to use you in ministry are two separate things—otherwise, how could people work miracles, prophesy, and cast out demons, yet hear Jesus say, "I never knew you" (Matthew 7:21-23)?

Of course, the healthier your relationship with Jesus, the more effectively you will convey His heart and character as you minister; but the point is that you don't have to wait to achieve some "level" before you can step out and minister healing.

I once saw Jesus use three hundred Kenyan schoolchildren to minister healing with one-hundred-percent results; and they had only been Christians for about five minutes! Jesus said, "These signs will accompany those who believe..." There was no other stipulation or requirement—no age limit, no prayer or fasting quota to meet, and no theological degree to hold. It was simply this: Believe.

Do you believe?

Prayer Starter:

- ❑ Thank the Lord for choosing you to represent Him despite your imperfections.
- ❑ Repent in your heart of any time that you allowed yourself to think that you're not worthy to have a ministry like that of Jesus, and thank Jesus for making you worthy by cleansing and transforming you with His blood.

❑ Pray for any Christian friends who seem to feel unworthy to minister to others in Jesus' name. Ask the Holy Spirit to assure them of their salvation and open their eyes to the reality that they are new creations in Christ.

Journal Experience:

Ask the Lord why He would use you to minister healing despite your imperfections. Write down a few thoughts that come to mind.

_____

_____

_____

_____

_____

_____

_____

_____

_____

_____

_____

_____

_____

_____

_____

_____

_____

_____

_____

Action Step:

Call, text, email, or write to a fellow Christian and encourage them that you believe God wants to use them to minister healing to others.

Supplemental Reading:
❑   Luke 9

SECTION 2:
The Price Jesus Paid

DAY 6
THE COMPLETE GOSPEL

Art Thomas

Paul said, "I did not come with wise and persuasive words of human wisdom but in a demonstration of the Spirit and of POWER." The Gospel is power. To preach half a Gospel is not the Gospel. To preach that God just saves is not the message. God saves, heals, restores, baptizes, delivers... That is the Gospel of Jesus Christ.

~ Nathan Morris

> **Matthew 10:7-8** — As you go, proclaim this message: 'The kingdom of heaven has come near.' Heal the sick, raise the dead, cleanse those who have leprosy, drive out demons. Freely you have received; freely give. (NIV)

The word "Gospel" means "good news." Jesus called it the "Gospel of the kingdom" (Matthew 24:14). A "kingdom" is anywhere that a king's authority is expressed. And while Jesus was clear that His

Father's kingdom was within His disciples (Luke 17:21), He also talked about that kingdom coming upon the people to whom we minister (Matthew 12:28 and Luke 11:20).

Whenever a person comes in contact with the kingdom of God, things change. People are healed, the dead are raised, demons flee, and hearts are transformed. We have the responsibility and privilege of expressing the kingdom that is within us so that it can come upon others. And our hope is that when a person experiences the goodness of God's active authority (healing them, raising them to life, or setting them free), they will choose to surrender their lives to the King who just touched them.

Admittedly, the "good news" of God's forgiveness — purchased by the blood of Jesus — is the best news ever! Countless people have given their lives to Jesus based on this news alone — and they should! That news is so good on its own that no miracle is needed to make it better.

But God has such compassion on the people of the world that He made a way for the best news ever to be even better! While the core of the Gospel is our future eternal salvation, the beauty of the Gospel is that it is relevant to us right now. In other words, we don't have to wait until we die to experience the goodness of God's kingdom. Even though we'll have to wait until we enter eternity to enjoy our glorified bodies, Jesus has provided for our complete wholeness here and now — body, soul, and spirit.

The Greek word for "salvation" can also be translated as "health." And the Greek word for "save" is sometimes translated "heal" — it means to make a person completely whole. Throughout Scripture, we see forgiveness and healing mentioned together (for example: Psalm 103:3, Matthew 9:2-7, James 5:14-16). This convinces me that the same blood of Jesus that purchased your eternal salvation also purchased your earthly salvation (think "physical healing and freedom from darkness"). All these things are the ministry of God's kingdom, and all of them are part of the good news we carry.

Prayer Starter:

❑ Worship Jesus as the King of Kings and Lord of Lords that He is. Tell Him how great you believe He is.

❑ Ask the Lord to convince you even more fully of the present-day reality of His kingdom.

❑ Pray for God's kingdom to come and His will to be done on earth, just like it is done in heaven. Ask for God's supernatural intervention in every circumstance you encounter so that you can partner with Him in making this world a little more like His heavenly kingdom (feeding the hungry, providing for the poor, healing the sick, preaching the Gospel, etc.).

Journal Experience:

Think of some earthly circumstance that you would consider to be "good news" — perhaps an engagement or pregnancy, free tickets to the Super Bowl (or the World Cup, for our international readers), being given a new car, etc.

In what ways would you go about telling people about that news? How would you spread the news in person, on social media, through writing, and so forth?

Action Step:

Choose one of the methods of "good news sharing" that you wrote down in your answer to the Journal Experience, and do that same thing today regarding the Good News of the kingdom! Use that same method to tell people about the goodness of God and the spectacular results of Jesus' sacrifice for our bodies, souls, and spirits.

Supplemental Reading:
❑   Acts 8:4-8

Day 7
He Bore Your Sickness

Jonathan Ammon

The reason people get healed is because of the stripes of Jesus. It's not based on how good I am or if the person deserves it… It's based on the finished work of Christ, which is an historical fact: Jesus was whipped. So the only reason people get healed is because God is fulfilling the cost of what Jesus bore for us. That's the only reason. We just happen to be the instruments that He uses when we agree with it and we're able to minister it. But it's all on Jesus; it has nothing really to do with us. We just get to take part in the Father's business.

~ Brook Potter

Matthew 8:16-17 — When evening had come, they brought to Him many who were demon-possessed. And He cast out the spirits with a word, and healed all who were sick, that it might be fulfilled which was spoken by Isaiah the prophet, saying: "He Himself took our infirmities and bore our sicknesses." (NKJV)

The placement of Matthew's quotation of Isaiah 53 is unusual because we know that Jesus paid the full price for our healing on the cross. Healing is in the atonement. Yet here Matthew states that Jesus' physical ministry on earth—before the atonement—was fulfillment of Isaiah 53.

Matthew gives us just enough details to imagine a vivid picture of the sun setting behind a mountain as crowds of the demon-possessed, the disease-ravaged, the crippled, scarred, lame, deaf, mute, and physically tortured were carried, dragged, and led to the compassionate Messiah. Matthew says that this was the fulfillment of Christ taking our infirmities and bearing our sicknesses. This was the beginning of Christ's atonement.

Christ's entire life and ministry was a substitution for our suffering, our sin, and our weakness. He laid His heavenly glory aside to humble himself and enter this earth as a child, live a human life filled with pain and sorrow, experience every part of human growth and life, and finally be tortured, abused, mocked, and executed for our sin (Philippians 2:5-8 and Luke 2:52). He entered into human pain. He entered into human sickness. When He saw leprosy, he touched it. He placed His hand into the shame and hopelessness of chronic disease, and His touch made every situation whole.

Though He was and is the King of Kings and Lord of Lords, He humbled Himself to a place where He had to tell mere demons to leave even though the whole world was held together by His word! Finally at the crucifixion, He bore every sickness, every disease, every infirmity and destroyed the root of all sickness, suffering, and pain by paying the price for all sin.

I had a major breakthrough in healing ministry when the Lord paralyzed me in prayer and opened my eyes to a vision of Jesus surrounded by clamoring crowds of the sick and diseased. He stood swarmed by desperation and disease, and one by one, He tenderly kissed each open sore, and His kisses healed. His love entered our sickness and carries it away.

Prayer Starter:

- ❑ Thank God for His incredible humility and love. Thank Him that He understands our pain and suffering, that He endured every blow and every pain. Thank Him that He understands and identifies with our weaknesses.
- ❑ Ask God to reveal Christ as the substitute for our sickness and disease. If you are struggling with any sickness or weakness, picture Jesus bearing it on the cross. Know that it belongs to Him.
- ❑ Picture the people you know who are suffering with sickness and disease. One by one in prayer, take them to Jesus watch Him take their condition on Himself. Ask Him to reveal how He absorbed their condition on the cross, and remember this the next time you minister healing.

Journal Experience:

How should we treat sickness and disease if Jesus took it all? How does this impact our ministry and service to others?

_____

_____

_____

_____

_____

_____

_____

_____

_____

_____

_____

_____

_____

_____

_____

_____

Action Step:

Are you owning an infirmity or sickness ("my diabetes," "my sciatica," etc.)? Give it to Jesus. He already bore it. Picture Jesus on the cross, see your condition there, and agree that there's no sense in both of you owning it! Similarly, do you know others who are owning their conditions? Today, tactfully encourage someone that Jesus bore his or her condition in love for them. Offer to pray for their healing.

Supplemental Reading:
❑   Philippians 2:1-11

Author's Note: Inspiration for this chapter came from Dr. Michael Brown's "I am the Lord Your Healer" audio class, available at AskDrBrown.org.

DAY 8
HE TOOK YOUR PUNISHMENT

Art Thomas

[Healing ministry] works because it was the heart of the Father, you know. It's in the atonement – to be restored – to be healed. God doesn't do things halfway, so if He's going to do it, He might as well do it all the way. That's why it works – because He works!

~ *Pete Cabrera, Jr.*

Isaiah 53:4-5 — Surely He has borne our griefs (sicknesses, weaknesses, and distresses) and carried our sorrows and pains [of punishment], yet we [ignorantly] considered Him stricken, smitten, and afflicted by God [as if with leprosy]. But He was wounded for our transgressions, He was bruised for our guilt and iniquities; the chastisement [needful to obtain] peace and well-being for us was upon Him, and with the stripes [that wounded] Him we are healed and made whole. (AMP)

Four men brought their paralyzed friend to Jesus, but the house where He was preaching was too full. With great faith, they climbed the roof with their helpless friend, dug a hole above the preaching Messiah, and lowered their friend down to the Lord's feet.

If I were in Jesus' sandals, I would have drawn the logical conclusion that these men brought their paralyzed friend to be healed—and I would have been right. But Jesus had His ear to the Father's heart. Rather than speaking to the man's physical condition, His first words were, "Son, your sins are forgiven."

Scripture doesn't give us any detail about why this had to come first, but it wouldn't surprise me if this man was protesting all the way to the Master, "Put me down! I deserve this condition! Don't you realize how much I've done wrong in my life to deserve this paralysis? I don't want to see that Holy Man! Put me down and let me reap what I've sown!"

Jesus looked at the man and said, "Son, your sins are forgiven." Without the man even repenting or confessing anything, Jesus forgave him. Then, to prove His authority to proclaim the Father's forgiveness, Jesus healed the man. (See Mark 2:1-12)

Many people think they're unworthy of healing. Perhaps their sickness or disease is the direct result of sinful addiction, sinful relationships, or other sinful decisions. One could rightly say that they deserve their condition, but the reality is that they actually deserve worse: death (Romans 6:23).

Nevertheless, Isaiah said that Jesus carried our sorrows and pains of punishment. If you think your wounds are because of your sin, I have good news: Jesus was wounded for your transgressions and bruised for your guilt and iniquities. If you think you need this punishment to bring peace and well-being to your life, I have good news for you: "the chastisement needful to obtain peace and well-being for us was upon Him." Jesus already took it all.

If you have put your faith in Jesus, there is no punishment left to endure. Jesus took it all. He says to you first and foremost today: "My son, My daughter, your sins are forgiven." But He doesn't stop there. His next command is to rise up and walk. Be healed in Jesus' name!

Prayer Starter:

- ❏ Thank the Lord for leaving no punishment for you to endure and for taking the full consequences of your sin.
- ❏ Tell the Father that you receive His complete and total forgiveness through Jesus' blood.
- ❏ Ask God to help you see the world through His eyes of forgiveness and to view others with the same compassion that caused Jesus to endure the cross.

Journal Experience:

Read Hebrews 12:1-11 about how the Lord disciplines His children. First, notice that the context is persecution and opposition from sinners (see especially verse 3). God uses opposition and hardship from the world to discipline us. The Greek word for "discipline" or "chastise" here refers to stern instruction and correction. It's the word used by Pilate when he argued with the bloodthirsty crowd, not wanting to do anything too severe to Jesus (Luke 23:16 and 22).

Knowing this, how would you explain the difference between punishment for sin (which Jesus took on our behalf) and discipline from the Lord (which is something we all endure from our loving Father)? What would you tell a person who believes that God gave them their sickness or disease as punishment for a previous sin?

_____

_____

_____

_____

_____

_____

_____

_____

_____

Action Step:

When Jesus sent His disciples out to heal the sick, He said, "Freely you have received; now freely give" (Matthew 10:8). You cannot give what you do not have. It is vitally important that we truly process the Lord's forgiveness on a personal level so that we can proclaim His forgiveness to others with conviction and authority.

One of the most important parts of processing your own forgiveness is personally forgiving others. (See Matthew 6:14-15, 18:21-35, and Luke 7:47.) Ask the Holy Spirit to make you aware of anyone you might need to forgive for any offense large or small. If someone comes to mind — perhaps a parent, spouse, co-worker, family member, church, neighbor, or anyone else — first receive the Lord's forgiveness as you repent of holding bitterness in your heart against that person or group. Second, recognize that everything you wish would happen to that person in response to their sin (and worse) has already happened to Jesus. Realize that forgiveness is impossible apart from the blood of Jesus paying the price. Ask Him to help you forgive the person or group who offended you based on the fact that He already suffered for their sin and His suffering was enough.

Lastly, realize that forgiveness is not a feeling or emotion; it is a choice based on the price Jesus already paid for sin. So voice out loud the following sentence: "I choose to forgive _____ for _____." Thank the Lord for setting you free from bitterness!

Supplemental Reading:
- ❑ Matthew 18:21-35
- ❑ Romans 5:1-11

DAY 9
BY HIS STRIPES WE ARE HEALED

Art Thomas

Jesus actually took the stripes for our healing — for the healing of our bodies. Because He did that, we know that's His heart; we know that's His desire. So all we're really doing is just releasing that revelation over people, and healing happens.

~ *Les Coombs*

> **Isaiah 53:5** — But he was pierced for our rebellion, crushed for our sins. He was beaten so we could be whole. He was whipped so we could be healed. (NLT)

First John 3:8 tells us that the reason Jesus came into the world was to destroy the devil's work. In context, this passage speaks of our freedom from sin; but the same results play out when it comes to sickness and disease. Jesus was clear in John 10:10 that stealing, killing, and destruction are the work of "the thief;" but He contrasted this, declaring, "I have come that they may have life, and have it to the full."

As you read a couple days ago, Jesus' atonement was technically carried out throughout His entire life, culminating in His death and resurrection. Prior to destroying the devil's work of sin by shedding His own blood for our forgiveness, Jesus was already actively engaged in destroying the works of the devil. He "went around doing good and healing all who were under the power of the devil..." (Acts 10:38).

Since Jesus healed every single person who came to Him, called out to Him, or had someone come to Him on their behalf, it's fair to assume that all sickness and disease is ultimately the work of the devil (because even if there is not a demon directly involved, the origin of sickness and disease can be traced back to the devil's work in the Garden of Eden, tempting mankind to choose sin over faith and obedience).

Even in cases where God causes a sickness (like Saul's blindness), it is still the devil's work (because Saul would not have been stricken blind if not for his own sinful, murderous rampage against the early Church) — and this is why healing was still the prescription for Saul's eyes. Jesus — both then and now — loves to destroy the devil's work!

What does all this have to do with the whipping of Jesus? Everything. The fact is, some people are not convinced that the whipping of Jesus specifically paid for physical healing. Perhaps the most compelling argument is that when Peter quoted Isaiah, his context could imply a metaphorical "healing" from sin (1 Peter 2:24). Personally, though, I don't see this as being too big of an issue. Everything Jesus did paid for everything sin did.

Everything Jesus did was to destroy the devil's work. By His stripes—by His wounds—by the beating, flogging, and torture He endured—He purchased us out of the dominion of darkness and brought us into His "good news" kingdom (Colossians 1:13-14). He saved us—body, soul, and spirit. He healed us spiritually, psychologically, emotionally, and even physically.

Everything Jesus did paid for everything that we have in the kingdom. Did the whipping Jesus endured produce our healing? Absolutely. *Everything* Jesus endured produced our healing. Whether Isaiah spoke literally or figuratively about Christ's wounds healing us, we know that our physical healing was purchased with the blood of Jesus. Why? Because the blood of Jesus destroys the devil's work (Revelation 12:11)!

Prayer Starter:

❑ Thank Jesus for the price He paid with His whole life—stepping out of heaven and humbling Himself all the way to the cross—so that you could be saved (body, soul, and spirit).

❑ Ask the Lord to partner with you in destroying all the devil's attempts to work in your life.

❑ Ask the Holy Spirit to help you see all sickness and disease as works of the devil that need to be destroyed so that Jesus can receive everything for which He paid.

Journal Experience:

Ask Jesus what He thinks about sickness and disease. Write down the thoughts that come to you.

_____

_____

_____

_____

_____

_____

_____

_____

_____

_____

_____

_____

_____

_____

_____

_____

_____

_____

Action Step:

Jesus has all authority (Matthew 28:18 and Philippians 2:9). His power is superior to all the power of the devil (Luke 10:19). So when His kingdom clashes with the kingdom of darkness, Jesus wins (Matthew 12:28)! The devil's work is not limited to sin or even sickness—it is anything that is contrary to the righteousness, peace and joy of God's kingdom.

Today, look for a work of the devil to destroy. This may mean praying for someone who is sick, or it may mean giving food to someone who is hungry. It may involve giving someone money or comforting someone who is mourning a loss. Whatever it is that you see to be the devil's work today, address it with the love and nature of Jesus with help from the Holy Spirit, and expect Jesus to shatter the work of the enemy.

Supplemental Reading:
- ❏ Colossians 1:3-23
- ❏ Revelation 12:7-12

DAY 10
HIS SACRIFICE WAS FOR THE WHOLE WORLD

James Loruss

When I go to a restaurant, and I pay for a meal, I want to get what I paid for. And I truly believe that Jesus wants to get what He paid for – that the cross was not in vain. But we are true beneficiaries of the FULL work of the cross – of everything that Jesus set out to accomplish. He desires that it will be fulfilled.

~ Michel Borchardt

> **1 John 2:2** — He is the atoning sacrifice for our sins, and not only for ours but also for the sins of the whole world. (NIV)

The blood of Jesus is potent and powerful. Think with me for a moment: By the shedding of one Man's blood, the sins of the whole world are paid for (Romans 5:19). We serve an amazing Savior! By His precious sacrifice, He paid the price for you: body, soul, and spirit.

But this sacrifice is not only for you; it is for

all. This doesn't mean everyone is going to heaven; but it does mean that the price for everyone has been paid, which proves the will of God (2 Peter 3:9).

During a prayer meeting at my church, the Lord gave me a vision that has changed the way I do ministry and the way I live my life. In this vision I saw a giant pool in front of me. In the pool I saw every family member and friend I knew that did not know Jesus. As I looked closer I could see that they were drowning and struggling to breathe. It was quite graphic. I began to break down, and I cried out, "God! Why are you showing this to me?" At that moment I saw Jesus standing next to me. He handed me a life-preserver and said, "This is My body which was broken for you and for them." Then I heard Him say something I will never forget. He told me, "My sacrifice is enough to save them, but YOU are the one who must throw the life-preserver."

That's when it hit me: God was waiting for me to move.

God is waiting for you to move. There's an entire world around you living in darkness! It's our job as Christians to see that Jesus receives what He already purchased 2000 years ago.

Remember that your life is not your own now. Second Corinthians 5:15 says, "And he died for all, that those who live should no longer live for themselves but for Him who died for them and was raised again." Every person you encounter should be extended the power and love of God simply because Jesus is worthy. He already paid the price for their forgiveness, healing, and freedom; and they need to know!

Prayer Starter:

- ❑ Thank Jesus for His sacrifice that paid for your complete wholeness: body, soul and spirit.
- ❑ Thank God for the incredible value He has placed on your life, and ask Him to help you understand how valuable you are to Him.
- ❑ Ask God for opportunities to express the forgiveness and healing that flow out of the sacrifice of Jesus—not simply for Christians, but for all humanity.

Journal Experience:

Write down three names of people you know who don't know (or have not accepted) the Good News that Jesus has already paid for their complete wholeness. Then write a short prayer asking the Lord to open their eyes to the truth.

_____

_____

_____

_____

_____

_____

_____

_____

_____

_____

_____

_____

_____

_____

_____

_____

_____

Action Step:

God is waiting for you to move. Every person you'll encounter has incredible worth to the Kingdom of God; otherwise the sacrifice of Jesus would have been for only a select few.

The price Jesus paid was for every person you'll see today. As you go about your day, ask the Holy Spirit to highlight at least one person for you to tell this good news.

If Jesus decided they were worth dying for, then they are certainly worth your time.

Supplemental Reading:
❑ Matthew 13:44-46
❑ Romans 10:14

SECTION 3:
Processing the Times When Nothing Seems to Happen

DAY 11
LOVE NEVER FAILS

James Loruss

It's when power and love come together that the Church will be unstoppable. I believe that our obligation is to love. I have a core value that it's impossible to pray and [have] nothing happen...if we're operating out of a place of love. If I've loved, something still happened.

~ *Chris Gore*

1 Corinthians 13:8a — Love never fails...
(NIV)

I remember when I first started in healing ministry. Everything was exciting! I watched people who could barely walk, now running around because God had just touched them. The list of healings and miracles went on and on. For a few months, my mind was always thinking about healing. I tried to find as many casts, canes, and walkers as I could!

One day the Lord showed me that I was more

excited about the healing than I was about Him as The Healer. The Holy Spirit gently showed me my enthusiasm was good but a little misguided. It's not about the healing. As Kristina Waggoner put it in our movie, physical healing is "a love language of God."

I've found that many people have the same experience I did when they begin to see the impossible happening through them. It's exciting to watch an impossible healing take place in front of your eyes! But did you know that love is also impossible apart from God? We need the Holy Spirit to enable us to truly love others (Galatians 5:22).

First John 4:19 says, "We love because He first loved us." The only reason we know how to love is because God first showed us how.

Operating in the supernatural is impossible apart from God — whether seeing healings or simply stopping to love someone. The good news is that if you're walking in His love, you cannot fail. It's impossible! I've found so much freedom in this thought when ministering to others. It takes away all the striving, stress, and burden to "get it right." I know that even if I pray for someone and don't see healing happen, it wasn't a failure because that person still encountered the love and compassion of Jesus (even if I couldn't bring His healing power). And that's the purpose anyway: to introduce people to Jesus!

Your job is to love. When you simply go out and love people, healings will naturally follow. But if you work incredible miracles without expressing the love of Christ, then you're wasting your life (1 Corinthians 13:2).

Prayer Starter:

- ❑ Thank God for His unfailing love for you.
- ❑ Repent of any time you've put healing above loving. Receive God's forgiveness and His empowerment to think differently.
- ❑ Ask God to reveal His love through you.

Journal Experience:

First Corinthians 13:8 says that "love never fails." Right before this, Paul gives a list that clearly describes love. God is love, so these traits describe Him too. But through knowing Christ, we have become one with Him in spirit (1 Corinthians 6:17), and that means we have become love too! His identity has become your identity because your old, sinful self has died (Galatians 2:20 and Colossians 3:3).

I believe that God wants to show you your identity in Him right now. Below is an adaptation from First Corinthians 13:4-8a in which every instance of the word "love" has been replaced with a blank line. On each line, write your first name:

_____ is patient, _____ is kind. _____ does not envy, _____ does not boast, _____ is not proud. _____ does not dishonor others, _____ is not self-seeking, _____ is not easily angered, _____ keeps no record of wrongs. _____ does not delight in evil but rejoices with the truth. _____ always protects, always trusts, always hopes, always perseveres. _____ never fails.

Now, read aloud the paragraph you just filled in, and allow the Lord to speak to your heart about your identity in Christ.

Action Step:

Look for a practical way to love someone today. Remember, love is not an emotion but is a decision to self-sacrifice for someone else. Look for a way to love someone without any concern for the results and without any strings attached. If an opportunity arises to pray or share the Gospel, go for it. But if not, remember that your assignment is simply to love them. Love never fails!

Supplemental Reading:
❑ Romans 6:5-14
❑ Ephesians 5:1-2

Day 12
Perseverance

Art Thomas

Sometimes it takes a little bit of time, and we just need to keep pressing in and pressing in and pressing in. And never quit. I was asked one time, "How long do I keep believing?" and I keep telling them, "Until you see the desired result – doesn't matter how long it is. Keep pressing in."

~ Tim Gingrich

Mark 8:22-25 — They came to Bethsaida, and some people brought a blind man and begged Jesus to touch him. He took the blind man by the hand and led him outside the village. When he had spit on the man's eyes and put his hands on him, Jesus asked, "Do you see anything?"

He looked up and said, "I see people; they look like trees walking around."

Once more Jesus put his hands on the man's eyes. Then his eyes were opened, his sight was restored, and he saw everything clearly. (NIV)

It was the last day of my first trip to Uganda. I was preaching in a small African town named Nnambo. I taught the people to minister healing, and then I wanted to demonstrate. I asked who in the meeting had eye problems. In the two weeks previous, I had witnessed about fifteen people healed of partial or complete blindness, so I was certain that it would work. Three people raised their hands, and I chose the woman closest to me.

"What is your problem?" I asked. Pastor Paul translated.

The woman was far-sighted and couldn't read.

Confidently, I placed my hands over her eyes, said, "Eyes, open in Jesus' name," and then opened a Bible for her to check for improvement.

"Any change?" I asked.

"No."

This didn't dissuade me. I had seen this happen enough times to know that God wanted it, and this wouldn't be the first time I tried more than once.

I placed my hands over her eyes again. "Eyes, open in Jesus' name." I opened a Bible. "Any change?"

"No."

This routine continued for fifteen minutes. There was no need to change the words I was saying because her healing had nothing to do with me saying the right words. And it wasn't a matter of me believing the wrong or right thing because I had all the confidence in the world that it would work (based on fifteen cases in the previous two weeks!).

Nevertheless, fifteen minutes passed, and the woman's condition hadn't changed in the slightest.

One woman in the church stood up and walked out. I was starting to lose them! I can't even explain all the confusion running through my mind. It must have been the same feeling the disciples had after healing the sick, multiplying food, and then being unable to cast a demon out of an epileptic boy (Luke 9).

Trying to keep others from walking out, I turned to the congregation and asked, "Did Jesus pay the price for this woman to see clearly?"

I waited for them to answer.

"Did He pay a very high price for her healing?"

The people stared at me, wondering where I was going.

"Then does it matter if I look like a fool up here in front of all of you while I keep trying over and over to see Jesus receive what He paid for?"

The tension was broken, some of the people smiled, and I placed my hands back on the woman's eyes. "Eyes open in Jesus' name." I opened the Bible. "Any change?"

"No."

This continued for five more minutes until suddenly she could read the large-print headings in her Bible. I still wasn't satisfied because Jesus paid for complete healing, but lunch was overdue, and I wanted these people to be able to eat.

"You see, this is working! I'm going to continue ministering to her until it is complete, but now you see how to do this: place your hands on the person, speak to the condition in Jesus' name, test it out, and continue the process until you see results."

I then invited all who needed healing to come forward. Ten people lined up. Then I invited the rest of the church to come pray for them while I returned to the woman with the eye problems. I placed my hands back on her eyes. "Eyes, open in Jesus' name." I opened the Bible. "Any change?"

She smiled and began to read everything.

That's not my favorite part of the story, though! As the woman went to sit back down, I asked Pastor Paul to stop her. "You can now go pray for someone else!"

The woman smiled even brighter and found the only man in the line to whom no one was yet ministering. He happened to be an old man who was completely blind.

Can you guess who the first person in that line of people was to be healed?

Every single one of them was healed, and I only ministered to the one woman.

If you minister to someone and don't see them healed, it's not a reflection on God's will. If Jesus had touched them, then they would have been healed. Scripture teaches us to be persistent. I have learned that every time I minister again in perseverance, I'm stepping into a new level of faith because I'm overcoming one more time that I didn't see results. While it takes a measure of faith to speak once to a condition and expect healing, it takes more faith to speak again after watching nothing happen the first time! So every time I try again, my faith is growing; and I know that eventually, I'll actually step into real faith and see results.

Jesus said that everyone who asks receives (Matthew 7:8). That means the only way to be certain that I won't receive something is to stop asking!

Prayer Starter:

❑ Describe to Jesus what you love about Him and what His sacrifice means to you.

❑ Ask the Holy Spirit to produce perseverance in you so that you will not be intimidated by a lack of visual results.

❑ Pray for someone you know who has been suffering with a sickness or disease for a long time. Ask the Lord to encourage them in their faith, and ask Him to give you the faith needed to see them experience a breakthrough.

Journal Experience:

Many times when I'm ministering to someone without seeing immediate results, the person seems to feel bad for me. They say things like, "It's okay...Maybe today isn't my day. There are other people who need you to pray for them. You don't have to keep going." In some cases, this is their polite way of asking me to stop praying, but I don't settle for that. I tell them, "If you want me to stop praying for you, then you're going to have to actually say so. Until then, I'm going to keep going after this like a pit bull because I want to see Jesus receive what He paid for."

Even still, I have occasional times when I notice that I'm starting to strive (by that, I mean I begin "trying harder" because I maybe want to be seen as powerful or because I'm feeling desperate for the person or because I'm starting to feel like I need to perform in order to gain God's attention). It doesn't happen a lot, but when it does, I know I've stepped out of faith and into works. Sometimes I can bounce back from this mindset and move back into simple trust in Jesus. Other times, I find myself emotionally worn out and unable to easily recover. That's a matter of weakness on my own part, but it's not uncommon for those of us who practice a lot of healing ministry.

In these times, I need to find a tactful way of backing out without implying that it wasn't God's will for the person to be healed. What would you say to a person you're praying for if you suddenly recognized that you were struggling to recover from weak faith and needed to take time away to pray and emotionally recharge?

Action Step:

Contact someone you know who has been suffering with a long-term condition, and offer to pray for them to be healed. Tell them what you believe about God's desire to heal them and the price Jesus paid to set them free. Then—whether in person, over the phone, or even in an e-mail—command them to be healed in Jesus' name and ask if they're feeling any improvement.

Supplemental Reading:
❏   Luke 11:5-10

DAY 13
LEAVING THE BURDEN WITH JESUS

James Loruss

I often – when I go back to my hotel after doing a healing meeting – am extremely grateful and extremely thankful for what I have seen; but there's another side of me that's just torn up for the ones who weren't healed. And I need to learn that it's not my glory when somebody gets healed, and it's not my burden when they don't. But that's still a process. I need to learn to take that burden to the cross. Just like I leave the glory with Him, I leave the burden with Him. But it still rips my heart for those that weren't healed.

~ *Chris Gore*

Colossians 3:2-3 — Set your mind on things above, not on things on the earth. For you died, and your life is hidden with Christ in God. (NKJV)

This is perhaps one of my favorite verses from the Bible. "Set your mind on things above." Why do you suppose Paul writes this? I believe it's because he knows that the thoughts we entertain and keep in our heads are the ones that will eventually produce our actions.

If I pray for someone and they don't experience healing, I have two routes I can take with my thoughts: The first is to keep my mind fixed on the problem, leading me further from Christ and from truth. The second is to keep my eyes fixed on Jesus, the author and finisher of my faith.

If we're not careful, our ministry can become all about seeing the healing and fixing our minds on that instead of on Christ, the Healer.

Am I saying that you should simply forget about the person you just prayed for who didn't get healed? Of course not! What I am saying is that this should drive you to Jesus, not away from Him.

Every time I don't see someone healed, I do what the disciples did when they couldn't heal the epileptic boy: I go to Jesus and ask, "Why didn't it work? I know if they had touched You, they would've been healed." Then I let the Holy Spirit speak, correct, and minister to me. I grow, I move forward, and I leave the emotional weight of the experience with Jesus (1 Peter 5:7). I always come back to fixing my mind on heavenly things. "People not being healed" is an earthly thing, not a heavenly thing. Fix your eyes on Jesus.

Jesus is the finisher (or "perfecter") of our faith (Hebrews 12:2). This means our faith is not yet finished or perfected and is still being worked out. He's working on you. He's working on me. And as we look to Him for our identities, we'll become more and more like Him.

Prayer Starter:

❑ Thank Jesus for carrying the weight of all our earthly struggles and failures so that we can live in joy and freedom.

❑ Thank God for what He's already done through you. If you're still reveling in the glory of someone being healed, defer that glory to Him by worshipping Him for what He did. And if you're carrying emotional weight for people you prayed for without results, cast that burden on Jesus and ask Him to help you stay focused on Him.

❑ Ask the Holy Spirit to help you be more impressed with heaven than you are intimidated by the world.

Journal Experience:

What do you understand heaven to be like? I'm not talking so much about physical properties (like streets of gold or gates of pearl), but what is the experience of heaven like? When a person is in heaven, how are their emotions affected? How are their thoughts influenced? How does being in heaven influence a person's attitude and actions?

Action Step:

Today, consciously set your mind on things above. Think about God in heaven. Think about the fact that there is no sickness, disease, or lack of strength in heaven. Philippians 4:8-9 says, "Finally, brothers and sisters, whatever is true, whatever is noble, whatever is right, whatever is pure, whatever is lovely, whatever is admirable—if anything is excellent or praiseworthy—think about such things. Whatever you have learned or received or heard from me, or seen in me—put it into practice. And the God of peace will be with you."

Supplemental Reading:
❑ Matthew 6:9-10
❑ James 3:17

DAY 14
TAKING RESPONSIBILITY

Jonathan Ammon

Very important – and I've seen this especially when it comes to failure – the responsibility falls on us. It's really easy to put it on God and say, "Well, it wasn't God's time; it wasn't God's will," and these other things. And we think that we're being spiritual by doing that because He's got really big shoulders and He can carry it. But for somebody who may have lost their daughter or some family member, if I blame God for that failure and I say, basically, "God killed your daughter because He didn't do something," that person's not going to want to have anything to do with God after that. And that's where I as a minister have to step forward and say, "No, it was me. I don't understand it. I don't know why. But, I didn't believe enough or I didn't 'something.' It's not God, because we know God's will." And that's a hard thing – it's a hard place to be for ministers of healing.

~ Brook Potter

Matthew 17:14-20 — When they came to the crowd, a man approached Jesus and knelt before him. "Lord, have mercy on my son," he said. "He has seizures and is suffering greatly. He often falls into the fire or into the water. I brought him to your disciples, but they could not heal him."

"You unbelieving and perverse generation," Jesus replied, "how long shall I stay with you? How long shall I put up with you? Bring the boy here to me." Jesus rebuked the demon, and it came out of the boy, and he was healed at that moment.

Then the disciples came to Jesus in private and asked, "Why couldn't we drive it out?"

He replied, "Because you have so little faith. Truly I tell you, if you have faith as small as a mustard seed, you can say to this mountain, 'Move from here to there,' and it will move. Nothing will be impossible for you." (NIV)

Imagine what the disciples must have felt when Jesus said, "Because you have so little faith." Here was a child being fiercely tormented by demonic power. His life was in danger. He had suffered for many years. His father was sobbing. You had commanded and prayed, but you saw no change. Instead, this child was thrashing on the ground in an epileptic fit, bound by the demon that refused to leave at your command. Now Jesus was telling *you* that all of the pain and suffering of that family could have been alleviated if only *you* had faith.

Jesus was clear that it was the disciples' unbelief at the root of their failure. There was no mystery as to why the boy was not healed. The disciples were responsible. He didn't single one out—any one of them could have had faith. The responsibility belonged to all of them collectively.

When my friend Kamal died of cancer, I knew he should have been healed. I could not blame the Father. Kamal was a Muslim. I knew that it was not God's will that any should perish (2 Peter 2:9). I was left with only one Biblical answer: my unbelief. I wrestled with that fact with tears. A man entered eternity unprepared because I failed to minister the power of God when it was mine to give. I was tortured by questions, "If I had prayed and fasted more, would Kamal be alive today? If I had confessed more Scripture, thanked God more, stood my ground harder..." Those questions are not gone completely. But my heart is whole; my vision of Christ is clear, and my faith unshaken.

I could have turned away from that truth, obscuring the pain by obscuring the revelation of God in Jesus. I could have cheapened the truth of the price Jesus paid by choosing to believe that God actually wanted Kamal to die in his sin. Instead, I pressed through the sorrow, found grace in my time of need, and determined in my heart that though I had lost Kamal, I would not lose another battle.

A year and half later, I saw cancer bow its knee to Jesus, and a man who would have died has life today because I took responsibility for my unbelief, pressed on, and grew in faith.

We, as the Body of Christ, need to take collective responsibility for healing ministry. The weight is too much of any single one of us to carry alone, but we are all responsible to represent Jesus. If we will humbly allow the Lord to correct us for our unbelief — even when it's emotionally painful — we will begin to see results rather than remaining the same.

Prayer Starter:

❑ Thank God for His incredible grace and love that no matter how we fall short, He loves us and treasures us the same. Thank Him for trusting us with a ministry to those who cannot help themselves.

❑ Ask God to help you hold on to the truth regardless of how it might hurt. Ask Him to help you take responsibility when it's yours to take while still leaving the weight of the burden with Jesus.

❑ Pray for the sick and dying in this world. Ask God to use you to bring them His healing. Ask Him to make you an open door for His power and to remove all obstacles to His healing power flowing freely through your life.

Journal Experience:

Has Jesus ever rebuked you for unbelief? How did/would you respond? How would Jesus want you to respond?

_____

_____

_____

Action Step:

Determine in your heart to never blame God for someone not being healed. If you have in the past, pray and apologize to God for making Him responsible for what was the falling short of our humanity. If you have prayed unsuccessfully for the sick in the past, consider verbally telling those people that you did not represent Jesus perfectly and that if you had, they would be healed right now. If you do this, offer to pray again for them.

Supplemental Reading:
❏   Acts 3:1-16

DAY 15
CARING FOR THE SICK
Art Thomas

One of the things I think about the human psyche is that we think if we push for one thing, we reduce the other — we have to somehow have a balance or whatever. But we have an abundant God; and so I can be 100% for medical intervention and 100% for supernatural, and I compromise neither.

~ Paul Manwaring

> **James 5:14-15** — Is anyone among you sick? Let them call the elders of the church to pray over them and anoint them with oil in the name of the Lord. And the prayer offered in faith will make the sick person well; the Lord will raise them up. If they have sinned, they will be forgiven. (NIV)

Notice that in James' instruction, it's "the prayer offered in faith" that will "make the sick person well" — not the oil that was smeared on the person.

Having been raised in a Pentecostal church, I've watched as Jesus-loving Christians treated olive oil like a magic potion. I myself carried a little vial of it in my pocket every day for several years!

Interestingly, I never saw anyone healed when I rubbed oil on them. One might think that James' words therefore weren't true, but then we remember that it's not the oil that heals the person; it's "the prayer offered in faith."

I smeared oil on the foreheads of perhaps a hundred people and never saw anyone healed; yet in the last three years, I've seen over two thousand people instantly healed without using oil even once.

So what, then, is the point of the oil?

Some scholars point out that in the culture of the New Testament, oil was rubbed on the sick for medicinal and cosmetic purposes. When Jesus told the parable of "The Good Samaritan," He said that when the Samaritan man saw the wounded and near-death Jewish victim, "He went to him and bandaged his wounds, pouring on oil and wine. Then he put the man on his own donkey, brought him to an inn and took care of him" (Luke 10:34). Here, oil was used as medicine; and in Matthew 6:17, Jesus instructed those who were fasting to put oil on their heads so that no one would know they were fasting (presumably making them look healthier).

Oil was used to soothe and care for the sick. Our opening Scripture passage is not a prescription for a magic potion or even a symbolic ritual; it's a practical instruction that as you pray for the sick, demonstrate the love of God by also caring for the sick.

Healing the sick is something that can only be done with faith, and we're all growing in that regard.

But caring for the sick is something we can do even when our faith is wavering. It's an expression of the gentleness and compassion of Jesus, bringing peace to the person's emotions and comfort to their bodies while we are simultaneously contending for their miraculous healing.

Caring for the sick is so important to Jesus that when He talked about the Final Judgment in Matthew 25:31-46, He praised the "sheep" for caring for Him while He was sick and condemned the "goats" for not caring for Him in His sickness. The "sheep" and "goats" each asked when they did such things, and each time, He answered, "Whatever you did for the least of these, you did to Me." In other words, when we one day stand before the Lord, He's not going to judge us for whether or not we ever healed the sick; but it seems we will have to answer for whether or not we cared for the sick.

As you minister healing to people, consider how your words and actions minister to the immediate needs of the person. Speak and act with the gentleness and compassion of Christ (especially when ministering to children since they are easily scared by some of our unnecessary antics).

Unless you are the person's medical doctor, never give any advice concerning his or her medical treatment. Leave the treatment of symptoms to the medical community; you deal with the spiritual realm. I never tell a person to stop taking medication without their doctor's approval and guidance.

Century-old teaching has convinced some that taking medicine shows a lack of faith, but I've seen far too many people miraculously healed while they were on medication to let that teaching persuade me. Even the woman with the issue of blood, who Jesus said was healed by her own faith, is said to have "suffered a great deal under the care of many doctors" (Mark 5:26).

Our role is to demonstrate the compassion of Christ by caring for the person's physical needs while simultaneously ministering healing in Jesus' name. That way, if our faith isn't perfectly like that of Jesus, the person will still have comfort and quality of life. And who knows? This care—and perhaps medication—might extend their lives long enough for us to step into the faith we need for their healing! Either way, Jesus will one day thank us for loving Him as we loved the sick.

Prayer Starter:

- ❑ Thank Jesus for the many ways He has shown His compassion toward you throughout your life.
- ❑ Ask the Lord to give you the strength and emotional fortitude to care for the sick while you persevere in ministering healing, and also ask Him to give you the faith you need to see more people healed instantly.
- ❑ Ask the Holy Spirit to help you demonstrate the compassion of Jesus toward others.

Journal Experience:

Imagine you're sick in bed with a terrible headache and cramping in your stomach. Then a Christian friend shows up at your house. How would you want them to approach you? Suppose they spoke words of healing over you but nothing changed. What would you want them to do next?

_____

_____

_____

_____

_____

_____

_____

_____

_____

_____

_____

_____

_____

_____

Action Step:

Look for someone who is sick or injured and do something practical for them—maybe holding a door for someone on crutches, buying cough drops for someone with a cold, or simply having a friendly conversation with someone in a wheelchair (instead of overlooking the person). After you have done something to tangibly minister kindness and compassion to the person, offer to pray for them.

Supplemental Reading:
❑ James 2:14-17

SECTION 4:
Overcoming Obstacles in Healing Ministry

DAY 16
DOUBTS, FEARS, AND INTIMIDATION

James Loruss (with Art Thomas)

I think some of the greatest roadblocks are doubt. You know, the doubts of, like, "Is it God's will?" "Is it God's time?" "Is it God's Heart?" ...They're lies that we hold on to. God's time was 2,000 years ago. God's will is now.

~ Chris Gore

2 Timothy 1:7 — For God has not given us a spirit of fear, but of power and of love and of a sound mind. (NKJV)

1 John 4:18 — There is no fear in love. But perfect love drives out fear, because fear has to do with punishment. The one who fears is not made perfect in love. (NIV)

You are power-filled (Acts 1:8), capable of loving like Jesus (John 13:34), and able to dispense peace (Luke 10:5-6). This is some of what God says about you whether you believe it or not. But how many times, when you're praying for someone, do you feel like the opposite is true?

Often when I am ministering healing, thoughts will run through my mind like these: "Why am I doing this? I look so silly. Does God even want to heal this person?" The list goes on and on.

You might ask, "Why do you keep going?"

Simple: I know what is right, and I know what Jesus paid for!

Much of spiritual warfare takes place in the mind. The enemy knows his best strategy against you is to make you doubt yourself and your identity in Christ, so that tends to be one of his chief strategies. As Cynthia Beckley pointed out in the film, the devil's first temptation of Jesus was a direct assault against His identity: "If you *are* the son of God..."

When we forget our identities, fear can set in. "What if it doesn't work?" "What if I say the wrong thing?" These are thoughts of your flesh, which are completely at odds with the Spirit (Galatians 5:17). It's nothing more than your human mind trying to avoid embarrassment and remain rational. Romans 8:6 says, "The mind governed by the flesh is death, but the mind governed by the Spirit is life and peace." As Brook Potter taught in our movie, thinking these thoughts isn't really doubt—only bowing to them is. We must be more impressed with Jesus than we are intimidated by the world around us.

The devil would love to force your mind off of Christ and onto the situation around you, so he uses the condition of the world to intimidate. As Jesus was walking on the water in Matthew 14:22-33, He called for Peter to join Him. Peter immediately jumped out of the boat to meet Jesus. "But when he saw the wind, he was afraid and, beginning to sink, cried out, 'Lord, save me!'" (v.30) Notice that it was not until Peter allowed the wind to intimidate him that he began to sink. Peter allowed himself to see the waves as being bigger than the Lord who called him to walk there.

So many times we let fear creep in by taking our gaze off of Jesus. We look at the storm surrounding us instead of realizing that Jesus calms every storm. We hear a word like "cancer" and suddenly feel helpless — as though cancer is a higher authority than Jesus! Fear has no place in your head; but when it comes (and it will), ask yourself whether Jesus is more or less powerful than the thing you fear. When I'm ministering healing, the only thing I concentrate on is Him and the price that is already paid. To quote Paul Manwaring, "God didn't send cancer to teach me a lesson. He sent Jesus to teach cancer a lesson." Jesus is more intimidating than any sickness or disease (Matthew 10:28). In the words of David, "The Lord is my light and my salvation — whom shall I fear? The Lord is the stronghold of my life — of whom shall I be afraid?" (Psalm 27:1).

Prayer Starter:

❏ Praise God for His power and love. Tell Him several things that you see Him to be more powerful than.

❏ Thank God for giving you a Spirit of boldness and peace. Ask Him to help you keep your eyes on Him when you minister.

❏ Pray that God reveals His peace through you as you minister so that other people are strengthened by your refusal to be intimidated by their condition.

Journal Experience:

First John 4:18 says that "perfect love drives out fear." Ask the Lord to tell you what He thinks of you. Write down some of the thoughts that come to mind.

_____

_____

_____

_____

_____

_____

_____

_____

_____

_____

Action Step:

Encourage someone in their faith today by encouraging them that Jesus is more powerful than the situation they're walking through. In order to avoid sounding cliché, share a testimony (either your own or one from someone else) that points to the power, ability, and love of God. Regardless of whether their situation has anything to do with healing, offer to pray for them so that Jesus can change their circumstances.

Supplemental Reading:
❑ Romans 8:11
❑ Hebrews 3:1

DAY 17
PRIDE

Jonathan Ammon

Many people will look to you. They'll say, "You're a healer. You healed me." But no. We point everybody to the Gospel — to Jesus Christ.

~ *Michel Borchardt*

> **James 4:6-7** — But he gives us more grace. That is why Scripture says: "God opposes the proud but shows favor to the humble." Submit yourselves, then, to God. Resist the devil, and he will flee from you. (NIV)

Pride is one of the most subtle and common stumbling blocks to operating well in the supernatural. Just after the disciples failed to cast the demon out of the epileptic boy, they were caught arguing about who would be the greatest. Jesus silenced them by placing a little child in their midst and teaching them that they must become like a child

(Luke 9:46-48).

After the seventy-two disciples returned from their ministry expeditions, they were rejoicing because they were able to cast out demons; but Jesus realigned their focus, saying that instead they should rejoice that their names are written in Heaven (Luke 10:17-20). He then rejoiced that God had hidden the miraculous from the wise and revealed it to "little children" (v.21).

Children know that they have no ability to feed, clothe, or care for themselves; instead, they are completely dependent upon their parents for everything. Without their parents, they are helpless. And they are completely comfortable and confident in that. In the same way, we have no ability in and of ourselves to accomplish anything. All power is in our Father's hands. This is good news because He is a loving Father whom we can trust completely. He wants all to be healed much more than we do!

Grace is the ability to do what we cannot do. When we believe we can do things in our own strength or because we possess something in and of ourselves, God allows us to fail. He opposes us. When we humble ourselves—acknowledging our need and completely trusting in His goodness and provision—we receive the supernatural ability to see the sick made whole.

Prayer Starter:

❑ Thank God for being a wonderful Father. Thank Him that He forgives all of our sins and heals all of our diseases (Psalm 103:3). Thank Him that He provides all that we need and never fails.

❑ Humble yourself before God. Acknowledge that you can do nothing without Him, but that with Him you can do all things. Ask Him to search your heart for pride. If He brings any to your attention, ask Him how to deal with that pride.

❑ Ask the Lord to lift Himself up and glorify Himself in your ministry to others. Ask that you could represent Jesus to others and that they would not give you any glory. Ask that Jesus would receive all the glory, honor, and praise.

Journal Experience:

What did humility and power look like in the life of Jesus? What needs to happen in your life in order for the humility of Jesus to be seen in your life, ministry, culture, and community?

_____

_____

_____

_____

_____

_____

_____

_____

_____

_____

_____

_____

_____

_____

_____

_____

_____

Action Step:

Meditate on how to redirect praise, glory, and honor to Jesus. Ask the Lord if there is anyone in your life whom you consider yourself to be "above" in ministry. Ask the Lord how you can practically and humbly serve them (not teach them, but *serve* them). Make a plan to do that in the next week.

Supplemental Reading:
❏ Matthew 5:3
❏ Luke 24:27
❏ Philippians 2:1-11

DAY 18
DISCOURAGEMENT

James Loruss

I've had some times when I've lost some big battles that I knew I was going to win. I know that. People close to me — and I've seen them go ahead and die, or they didn't get healed... And what I try to do is I look at everything as there are two kingdoms at war, and there are great soldiers who die in war, and you don't have to win every battle. But...my job is to believe and heal.

~ Art Montgomery

Matthew 14:10,13-14 — So John was beheaded in the prison... As soon as Jesus heard the news, He left in a boat to a remote area to be alone. But the crowds heard where He was headed and followed on foot from many towns. Jesus saw the huge crowd as He stepped from the boat, and He had compassion on them and healed their sick. (NLT)

Put yourself in Jesus' shoes here. Your close relative was just killed for his faith, and all you want to do is get away. You need time to grieve—to process, to just be alone. Jesus could have explained to the crowd what happened and how He needed time. They would certainly understand, right? Amazingly, we see Jesus put His needs aside and selflessly act in compassion.

Not too long ago, close family friends of mine went through a very difficult season. One of their family members was diagnosed with cancer. I watched as with each report they continually looked to God and never waivered in their trust that He is able to bring healing. Art and I prayed with him too and believed for his healing; but in the end, he died from the cancer.

This was hard to process emotionally. Watching so many people who were close to me walk through this difficult situation, I realized that as fun and exciting as healing ministry can be, it still has its sobering moments. Faced with a painful circumstance where I saw a different outcome than what I believe God desired, I had to make a decision: Am I going to stop praying for people because it's just too hard? Or, like my Savior who saw the crowds, will I move beyond the pain in my heart, step from the boat to the land, and compassionately continue to pray for the sick?

Why do you suppose Jesus didn't stay in the boat? It would have been totally understandable for Him to simply be alone for a time. I don't fully understand it myself. All I know is that I want to be like Him.

As you minister to the broken, the hurting, and the dying, you will very likely encounter hardships. What will you choose to do in those trying moments? Will you step out again?

Prayer Starter:

- ❑ Praise God for His faithfulness and His ability to turn any situation around for our good.
- ❑ Ask the Lord to give you compassion that transcends emotional exhaustion or earthly circumstances.
- ❑ Pray for people you know who have seen their loved ones die of sickness and disease. Ask the Lord to strengthen them in their faith and help them to believe for future testimonies.

Journal Experience:

What would you say to a person who prayed, believing, for a loved one to be healed of a terminal illness yet saw that loved one die? Remember to think about such things as tact and gentleness in your approach.

_____

_____

_____

_____

_____

_____

_____

_____

_____

_____

_____

_____

_____

_____

_____

_____

_____

_____

Action Step:

Today, I want you to simply rest. Take 3 minutes right now to rest in God's presence. Focus on the goodness of God and thank Him for His faithfulness. All your peace, strength, and joy come from Him. For this next brief moment, forget about everything you have to do today and just allow yourself to become aware of His presence.

Supplemental Reading:
❑ Psalm 100:4
❑ Joshua 1:9

DAY 19
OTHER CHRISTIANS WHO
DISAGREE WITH YOU

Jonathan Ammon

[One of the greatest difficulties is] from the Body of Christ — the people that assault you on a daily basis for believing that God is good and wants to heal people. To me, that's goofy, and it's almost laughable, but in another sense, it's so sad. Jesus did so much to accomplish what He did for us, and then — not only for you to not receive it, that's fine, it's your choice — but then when you want to get mad at someone who wants to see people go free that Jesus paid for to be free, that's frustrating. That's hard.

~ Josh Greeson

Mark 3:1-6—Another time Jesus went into the synagogue, and a man with a shriveled hand was there. Some of them were looking for a reason to accuse Jesus, so they watched Him closely to see if He would heal him on the Sabbath. Jesus said to the man with the shriveled hand, "Stand up in front of everyone."

Then Jesus asked them, "Which is lawful on the Sabbath: to do good or to do evil, to save life or to kill?" But they remained silent.

He looked around at them in anger and, deeply distressed at their stubborn hearts, said to the man, "Stretch out your hand." He stretched it out, and his hand was completely restored. Then the Pharisees went out and began to plot with the Herodians how they might kill Jesus. (NIV)

Mark 9:14—And when He came to the disciples, He saw a great multitude around them, and scribes disputing with them. (NKJV)

Jesus was angered by the stubborn unbelief and legalistic lack of compassion in the hearts of His accusers. He was perfect in every way, yet He was still angered, distressed, and maybe even frustrated by the unbelief and twisted perspectives of those around Him. He was the answer to the suffering, pain, and sin of the world — He perfectly demonstrated God's power and love — yet they still refused to see.

Many prefer argument and debate about God's power to heal over seeking God's power to heal. Some may have real questions and honest hearts that seek the truth. They need answers—truth, spoken in love and understanding. It is worth engaging the skeptic who is turning towards God, and we must demonstrate Christ's willingness to engage religious but honest seekers like Nicodemus.

But we must also keep in mind that many have formed their theology out of wounds and are simply seeking to confirm their unbelief.

When Jesus came down from the mount of transfiguration in Mark 9, He found His disciples arguing with the scribes; a heated debate was underway. The source of the debate was the disciples' failure to drive the demon out of the epileptic boy. A lack of results leads to debate.

Suddenly the scribes had ammunition to accuse and undermine Jesus' teaching and identity. Suddenly the disciples had the need to defend themselves. The failure to see results led to debate, argument, and strife; but all of that disagreement could have been silenced by casting the demon out of the boy.

Jesus did not enter the argument and assert all the right answers. Instead He cast the demon out of the boy, demonstrating the reality of God's power and answering His disciples' genuine questions in private later (Mark 9:28).

Demonstrate the power of God. Handle lack of results with humility and perseverance. Save the debate for those who are honestly seeking answers.

Prayer Starter:

- ❑ Thank God that He responds to us, loves us, and helps us in spite of our limited understanding.
- ❑ Ask God for humility, love, and understanding when dealing with those who disagree with you. Ask Him for compassion for those who have suffered and lost loved ones who were not healed. Ask for discernment for when to give

answers and engage in debate and when to move on.

❑ Pray for those who disagree with you. Ask God for His heart for them. Ask God to open their eyes. Ask Him to give you the words to say. Ask how you can bless them and bring them one step closer to Jesus.

Journal Experience:

How did Jesus respond to those who disagreed with Him about healing? How would He respond to those who might disagree with you now? How can you follow and imitate Jesus in this regard?

_____

_____

_____

_____

_____

_____

_____

_____

_____

_____

_____

Action Step:

Make a list of people who you have discussed or debated healing with in the past. Ask God what the next step should be in those discussions. Allow Him to speak to you about what discussions to continue and which ones to end. If you can't think of any disagreements or discussion regarding healing ministry, ask Him to lead you in bearing witness to the truth of Christ the Healer in the future.

Supplemental Reading:
❏   Mark 9:14-29
❏   Luke 13:10-17

DAY 20
BEING OVERWHELMED BY THE GREAT NEED AROUND YOU

Jonathan Ammon

When I go into Walmart, I see every single person who has a cane, every single person who has a cast, every single person on a motorized scooter – and each one of them draws my attention. It's painful for me sometimes to go out into public because I see all of the affliction, and I feel a responsibility to bring healing to every one of those people. And that is an extremely difficult burden. But at the same time [I'm] struggling with what the Bible says – that he who gives should not give begrudgingly. Ministering healing should not be done out of this begrudging "I have to." Ministering healing should be done because we want to, and we get to serve Jesus, and we get to love Jesus by loving these people and bringing his power into their lives
~ JonMark Baker

John 5:1-9a,13 — Some time later, Jesus went up to Jerusalem for one of the

Jewish festivals. Now there is in Jerusalem near the Sheep Gate a pool, which in Aramaic is called Bethesda and which is surrounded by five covered colonnades. Here a great number of disabled people used to lie—the blind, the lame, the paralyzed. One who was there had been an invalid for thirty-eight years. When Jesus saw him lying there and learned that he had been in this condition for a long time, He asked him, "Do you want to get well?"

"Sir," the invalid replied, "I have no one to help me into the pool when the water is stirred. While I am trying to get in, someone else goes down ahead of me."

Then Jesus said to him, "Get up! Pick up your mat and walk." At once the man was cured; he picked up his mat and walked...

The man who was healed had no idea who it was, for Jesus had slipped away into the crowd that was there. (NIV)

Jesus has more compassion than all of us, yet He did not pray for every sick person He saw. At the pool of Bethesda, He only healed one paralyzed man among a crowd of "the blind, the lame, the paralyzed." The King of compassion and mercy walked away from a whole crowd of those in need.

Jesus—though fully God—came as a human being just like you and me; He took on human limits (Philippians 2:6-8). Even Jesus could not physically handle all of the need around Him—it wasn't uncommon for crushing crowds to press in on all sides. I'm sure the demand carried an emotional weight as well.

Jesus had a mission to accomplish. He had only three short years to reveal the Father's heart, go to the cross, and rise from the dead. He had to be led by the Holy Spirit in order to know when to stop for the sick and when to move to the next city for the lost sheep who needed the message of life.

In the same way, we have a limited human capacity, a calling, and a mission to accomplish. Most of us are not called to go to the hospital every day and pray for the sick all day long. We all know that salvation of the soul is more vital than that of the body, yet most of us do not preach salvation to every person we see. The need is too overwhelming. We need a focus for how to handle the great need around us, and this can be found in our mandate in the Word of God, our calling within His body, and the leading of the Spirit.

These are not excuses to leave the sick behind! Most of us are not wearing ourselves out praying for the sick. This is the only story where Jesus explicitly passed people by without healing them. Most of us need to pray for strangers *more* often rather than *less* often. We are commanded to heal the sick and even to take responsibility for the sick in our city (Luke 10:9). We do that most effectively by allowing the Holy Spirit to direct us within that mandate and by answering the call of compassion. If we do that, He will protect our hearts from the paralyzing need around us and help us to remain effective in obeying Jesus' command to heal the sick.

Prayer Starter:

- ❑ Thank God for His incredible mercy that He left the 99 to go after us. Thank Him for His grace that covers all of the ways we fall short, all of our limitations, and all of our weaknesses.
- ❑ Ask the Lord to increase your compassion and open your eyes to the need around you. Ask Him to give you assurance of your calling, and to lead you to respond to the need of the world. Ask Him to give you assurance and confidence in His direction to reach out to the sick.
- ❑ Pray for the entire Body of Christ to be awakened to healing ministry so that we can all carry this ministry together and bear the load in a healthy way.

Journal Experience:

Even Paul, who saw every single sick person on the island of Malta healed (Acts 28:8-9), had to leave his friend Trophimus sick in the city of Miletus so that he could carry on with his mission (2 Timothy 4:20).

What practical advice would you give someone who is compassionate like Jesus and yet also finds himself or herself distracted or overwhelmed by that compassion? How would you encourage that person to remain "on mission" like Jesus?

_____

_____

_____
_____
_____
_____
_____
_____
_____
_____
_____
_____
_____
_____
_____
_____
_____
_____
_____
_____
_____
_____
_____
_____
_____
_____

Action Step:

Ask God to tell you right now who He would like you to minister to today. He might give you a specific name or a condition or perhaps even where to find the person (like when He sent Ananias to Saul in Acts 9:10-16). Write down the conditions, instructions, or "clues" that come to mind. Keep your eyes open for these people today and even in the days ahead. While you are looking for these people, allow yourself to pray for others as you are moved by compassion.

Supplemental Reading:
❑   Mark 7:24-30
❑   Mark 10:46-52

SECTION 5:
Some of the Ways
God Heals

Day 21
Who Needs to have Faith?

Jonathan Ammon

One of the traditions that we have in the Church is that the person you are praying for needs to have faith to be healed; and we say, "It's great if they have faith!" And Paul acknowledged that — you know, he saw someone that had faith to be healed, and he said, "Rise." But the responsibility really lies on the person ministering. So apart from laying hands, we sometimes have the responsibility to have the faith for them.

~ Brook Potter

Matthew 17:18-20 — Jesus rebuked the demon, and it came out of the boy, and he was healed at that moment.

Then the disciples came to Jesus in private and asked, "Why couldn't we drive it out?"

He replied, "Because you have so little faith. Truly I tell you, if you have faith as small as a mustard seed, you can say to this mountain, 'Move from here to there,' and it will move. Nothing will be impossible for you." (NIV)

Jesus did not address the child's faith. He did not address the father's faith. They were not the ones who had walked with Him and been trained by Him. It was the disciples who were responsible to bring God's deliverance to the boy. Jesus expected them to have faith for others who had none.

Today we are the disciples of Jesus. Today we are expected to have faith for others. Jesus never turned away someone seeking healing by saying, "You don't have enough faith to be healed." He acknowledged people's faith when they had it; but Lazarus didn't have faith to be raised from the dead, nor did the invalid at the pool of Bethesda, nor any other number of examples. In these cases, Jesus had faith for them. The responsibility for faith belongs to the disciples of Jesus.

This is good news! I have seen Muslims, Hindus, and cessationists (Christians who do not believe in present-day miracles and supernatural gifts) healed by the power of God when they had no faith to receive it. They did not have faith for themselves, but I believed God loved them and paid for their healing as well. No amount of unbelief in the world is more powerful than a believer's faith!

Many argue that unbelief prevented Jesus from healing in His hometown in Mark 6:1-6, but He did heal a few sick people even though the crowds were offended at Him. When crowds are offended by you, they usually do not let you lay hands on them. It is far more likely that those few sick people came to Him while the rest simply walked away.

Not only did Jesus say that the epileptic boy was not healed because of the disciples' unbelief, but He then stated that mountains move with even a small amount of faith. Many will argue that they had plenty of faith but that the mountain did not move (or that the sick were not healed) for some other mysterious reason. But Jesus' perfect faith-walk with the Father always produced results; He had no "mysterious reasons" hindering His ability to minister healing. Jesus said that faith moves the mountain, and His ministry was always effective.

The evidence of faith is a mountain moving. Feeling or thinking a certain way is not proof of faith. Faith in the name of Jesus heals the sick (Acts 3:12). If we see a lack of results, then we need to allow the Lord to deal with our lack of faith (just as He dealt with the disciples when they couldn't bring freedom to the epileptic boy). Otherwise, the condition of our faith will remain stagnant, and we will have nothing to offer the next person to whom we minister.

Only believe!

For a more complete description of what it means to have faith, see "Appendix C: The Difference Between Faith and Belief" on page 319.

Prayer Starter:

❑ Thank God for making a way for all to receive healing in Jesus name. Thank Him for trusting us with a ministry to those who cannot help themselves.

❑ Ask the Lord to open your ears to hear the truth about faith and healing. Ask Him what needs to change in your heart, mindset, or life. Ask Him what faith looks like.

❑ Talk to the Lord and make a determination with Him to have faith for others. Ask him to give you boldness to heal people who do not believe and do not expect healing.

Journal Experience:

Is there anything about this lesson that might change the way you minister? How would Jesus want you to personally process times when you don't see results?

_____

_____

_____

_____

_____

_____

_____

_____

_____

_____

_____

_____

_____

Action Step:

Make a plan to pray for an unbeliever for healing today or this week. Unbelievers have no faith in Jesus Christ, and you can have faith for them. Ask Jesus for boldness. Also, make a plan to pray for a Christian you know who is a skeptic regarding physical healing.

Supplemental Reading:
- ❏ Mark 16:15-18
- ❏ Acts 3:1-21
- ❏ Luke 9:1-6

DAY 22
AUTHORITY

Art Thomas (with Jonathan Ammon)

We have the fullness of God inside of us. So that power that raised Jesus from the dead lives inside of us and so we just need to constantly remember that... There's that scripture that says as He is so are we on this earth, and so, just [remember] that. He's given us all power and authority to cancel the works of the devil.

~ Kami Flack

Ephesians 2:6-10 — And God raised us up with Christ and seated us with him in the heavenly realms in Christ Jesus, in order that in the coming ages he might show the incomparable riches of his grace, expressed in his kindness to us in Christ Jesus. For it is by grace you have been saved, through faith—and this is not from yourselves, it is the gift of God—not by works, so that no one can boast. For we are God's handiwork, created in Christ Jesus to do good works, which God prepared in advance for us to do. (NIV)

After Jesus secured victory over sin and death through His sinless life, execution, and resurrection, "God exalted Him to the highest place and gave Him the name that is above every name" (Philippians 2:9). Jesus sat down at the right hand of the Father (Mark 16:19). The throne Jesus was given is one of absolute authority with direct access to the Father at all times.

According to Ephesians 2:6, we — as believers — have been seated on that same throne with Jesus. His absolute authority has been granted to us within the context of closeness to the Father (at His right hand).

Jesus' throne is established by the Father — it is the throne of a Son — and we who share in His victory are welcomed to sit on that throne with Him (Revelation 3:21). By receiving Jesus and believing in His name, we have been given the right to be called sons of God (John 1:12). Our authority is not merely something delegated to an outsider; it is something bestowed by a Father upon His own children.

True authority is directly related to one's relationship with God as "Father" because only from this relationship do we begin to speak as "sons." (Stick with me, ladies...the "sonship" thing applies to you too because it speaks of the privileged relationship we have all been given through Jesus, whether male or female.) Apart from this sonship, miracles are considered evil and sinful (Matthew 7:22-23); but within the context of this sonship (through union with Jesus), we will bear much fruit for the Kingdom as the Father backs up our prayers (John 15:1-17).

Notice how Jesus sent out His disciples before

leaving this earth: "All authority in heaven and on earth has been given to Me. Therefore go..." (Matthew 28:18-19). Jesus sent His disciples with the assurance of His absolute authority, granted from the Father. He sent His followers out in His name and with His divine command to stomp on every work of the devil.

As sons of the Most High God, sitting with Jesus on His heavenly throne, we live, do business, and minister under the highest Authority. As men and women under authority, we can give commands with the supreme rule and jurisdiction of the One who sent and commissioned us (which is what the centurion recognized was true about Jesus when he sent for the Lord to heal his servant in Luke 7:6-8). You have authority because you are a son of Almighty God—born of His Spirit because of the blood of Jesus.

The nature of our union with this King is that our words are capable of carrying the same weight as if Jesus Himself were to One to speak them. The words we speak emanate from the throne of Jesus because we are seated with Him there. They are authorized by the Father—*our* Father—and have supreme weight in the spiritual realm.

When you are submitted to God (under His authority as a son), the devil flees from you (James 4:7). Sickness and disease are no match for a son who knows his (or her) authority in Christ!

If I speak a word of authority to a sickness or disease (like when Jesus rebuked the fever from Peter's mother-in-law in Luke 4:39), my expectation must be that it will leave. If that thing does not leave, my first action is to speak to it again—even Jesus had to command a demon to leave more than one time

(Mark 5:8). But if I have done all that I know to do and have persevered for some time without results, then I need to examine whether or not I have been submitting to God as my Father.

I'm not saying that His Fatherhood or my sonship are in question — I'm saying that my rightful submission to Him as His son is in question, which — to the enemy — brings my authority into question. If I'm not submitted to God, am I really speaking on His behalf? One does not need to be perfect in order to minister with authority, but one does need to have a heart that is tenderly yielded to the will of the Father, desiring to please Him alone.

Immediately before James wrote that the devil will flee when we are submitted to God, he quoted Scripture saying, "God opposes the proud but shows favor to the humble" (James 4:6-7). God is not afraid to oppose prideful children. Sometimes God's mercy will overlook my shortcomings and heal the person anyway, so I don't assume I'm perfect when things do work out. But sometimes His love for me as His son overlooks the "ministry opportunity" because He wants to train me to represent Him well and become even more effective in the future (Hebrews 12:4-12).

When we humbly allow God to father us, His favor is released to accomplish the miraculous through our lives. Humble yourself before the Father. Be convinced in your heart and mind of the position you've been given in Christ — humbly recognizing God's amazing grace and the fact that you do not deserve it in the least. Speak with the authority you have been given — the authority of Jesus. Command sicknesses and diseases to leave people in Jesus' name. You're sure to see results.

Prayer Starter:

- ❑ Thank the Father for giving you the right to be called His son. Thank Him for giving you access to the same relationship with Him that Jesus presently has.

- ❑ Ask the Holy Spirit to examine your heart and expose any areas where you're walking in pride. Ask Him to correct those things in you and repent of any self-centeredness of which you become aware.

- ❑ Ask the Lord to help you set a good example of sonship for your fellow believers, and ask Him to help you do it humbly and like Christ, honoring others above yourself.

Journal Experience:

Consider the life of Jesus as revealed in the four accounts of Matthew, Mark, Luke, and John. Jesus expressed His authority in many ways—healing people with commands, calming storms, multiplying food, teaching powerfully, correcting sin, forgiving sin, and more. In the midst of all these things, Jesus remained in perfect humility, submitted to His Father. Using Jesus as an example, what do you think is the difference between humble confidence and prideful confidence?

_____

_____

_____

_____

_____

_____

_____

_____

_____

_____

_____

_____

_____

Action Step:

In the account of the centurion asking Jesus to heal his servant, we see a situation where Jesus ministered healing from a distance. The same thing happened with the Syrophoenician woman who came on behalf of her daughter (Mark 7:24-30). As you'll see in the next lesson, authority is one of the tools Jesus has given us for ministering healing, and it is a tool that does not require physical proximity to a person. All that is required is that in submission to God as Father, we speak on Christ's behalf and expect the results to happen as though Jesus Himself were the one who had spoken. Today, try to minister healing from a distance. Think of someone you know who has a sickness or disease, and — without them even knowing — speak to the condition as though the person is right there with you. Afterward, contact that person to tell them that you just prayed for them. Ask if anything has changed.

Supplemental Reading:
❑   John 15:1-17

DAY 23
PHYSICAL CONTACT (POWER)

Art Thomas (with Jonathan Ammon)

I have a very passive role in this. My goal is to put my hands there, and that's it. I don't have to say the right words or the right prayer or get it all just right. I just have to do what He said: put my hands there.

~ *Joshua Greeson*

> **Luke 6:17-19** — He went down with them and stood on a level place. A large crowd of his disciples was there and a great number of people from all over Judea, from Jerusalem, and from the coastal region around Tyre and Sidon, who had come to hear him and to be healed of their diseases. Those troubled by impure spirits were cured, and the people all tried to touch him, because power was coming from him and healing them all. (NIV)

When Jesus sent out His twelve disciples in His name, He gave them two tools for the purpose of casting out demons and curing diseases: power and authority (Luke 9:1). While these tools often work in conjunction, we do see cases where one or the other was used to minister healing on its own. For example, when the woman with the issue of blood touched Jesus' garment, no word of authority was spoken; but Jesus stopped because, at the moment of contact, He "realized that power had gone out from him" (Mark 5:24-34). And as you saw yesterday, a centurion sent word to Jesus that his servant was sick; but while Jesus was on the way, the centurion sent word that Jesus only needed to "say the word" based on the fact that He was a Man of authority (Luke 7:1-10). No physical contact took place, but the servant was healed through authority.

Generally speaking, "power healings" happen through physical contact (you'll read about the exceptions in a couple days). This is surely why Jesus specified that "those who believe" would "lay hands on the sick" and see them recover (Mark 16:17-18). Jesus Himself regularly healed people through physical contact (See Matthew 14:35-36, Mark 6:56, and Luke 4:40).

This power of the Holy Spirit goes beyond His indwelling presence. In the Old Testament, the Holy Spirit occasionally came "upon" people for various tasks—for example: prophesying (1 Samuel 10:10), winning battles (Judges 14:19), leading people (Numbers 11:17), and ministering miracles and prophecy (2 Kings 2:15). In every case that the Holy Spirit came upon people, He produced results in the natural realm that a person could not have accomplished in their own ability. In the New

Testament, however, the Holy Spirit came to live within people (John 14:16-17). After Jesus died and rose again, He breathed on His disciples and told them to receive the Holy Spirit (John 20:21-22). Many believe that this is the moment when the disciples received their "born-again" experience. Nevertheless, He also told them to wait in Jerusalem until the Holy Spirit had come *upon* them as well (Luke 24:49 and Acts 1:3-8). The Holy Spirit comes *within* us to transform us and make us more like Jesus; He comes *upon* us to transform the world around us.

It is possible to minister healing without the Holy Spirit's power *upon* you if you use authority. As a believer, you have the Spirit of sonship dwelling within you, granting you the authority of a son (Romans 8:15-16)! But authority is not the only tool Jesus gave His disciples. He gave us something far greater: His own Spirit—not merely dwelling within us (as incredible as that is on its own) but also clothing us with power for ministry!

This saturation with His Spirit's power is so important that Jesus trumped the Great Commission (to "go into all the world") with a command to "stay in this city" and wait for power (Luke 24:49 and Acts 1:4). He wants us to be completely inundated with His Holy Spirit—not merely containing Him within ourselves. Yes, we can effectively minister to others if we only have Him within us; but we will never be truly Christ-like unless we also have His Spirit upon us—empowering us to do things that are beyond our natural ability. Even the Lord Jesus—who arguably had the Holy Spirit within Him all His life—did not begin His earthly ministry until the Spirit had also descended "upon" Him like a dove (Matthew 3:16, Mark 1:10, Luke 3:22, and John 1:32).

If you look up the word "power" in the Bible, no one had healing power flowing through them more than Jesus. We should desire to be like Him. In fact, the Bible teaches that "whoever claims to live in Him must live as Jesus did." (1 John 2:6). Living and ministering like Jesus is not an option for the believer; it is a mandate.

Entire crowds were healed by power as a normal part of Jesus' ministry (Mark 6:56 and Luke 6:18-19). He regularly laid hands on people and healed them. And Jesus promised that those who believe in Him would do the same things and greater (John 14:12). If you want to be like Jesus, then you too need the Holy Spirit to operate more than *within* you for your own salvation—you also need Him to be *upon* you with power for ministry!

Prayer Starter:

❑ Thank God for pouring out His Spirit and the Spirit's power upon all (Joel 2:27). Ask Him for a fresh flow of power today.

❑ Read Acts 2:1-4, Acts 10:44-48, and Acts 19:1-7. If you have never had an experience with the Holy Spirit's power like the disciples in those passages, ask Jesus to baptize you in His Holy Spirit and wait for Him to do so.

❑ Ask God to regularly release His power to heal the sick through you. Ask Him for opportunities to lay hands on sick people. Ask Him for the words you need in order to explain what happened to a person after they are healed by His power.

Journal Experience:

Shortly after beginning His ministry, Jesus visited His hometown and attended one of the synagogue meetings. There, a scroll from the prophet Isaiah was handed to Him, and He read it out loud. It described purposes for which the Holy Spirit had come upon Him; and Jesus unashamedly rolled up the scroll and declared, "Today, this scripture is fulfilled in your hearing" (Luke 4:16-21). The ramifications for us became clear when Jesus later declared to His disciples, "As the Father has sent me, I am sending you" (John 20:21). His mission became our mission.

Below you will find the text of Isaiah's prophecy as Jesus read it in Luke 4:18-19 (NIV). In each line where the prophet wrote the word "me," you'll find a blank line. Write your first name into each blank and then read the words out loud, realizing that the Holy Spirit comes on us for the same reason He came on Jesus: Mission.

The Spirit of the Lord is on _____,

because he has anointed _____ to

proclaim good news to the poor. He has sent

_____ to proclaim freedom for the

prisoners and recovery of sight for the blind,

to set the oppressed free, to proclaim the year

of the Lord's favor.

Action Step:

Determine to make physical contact a part of your ministry to the sick. The next time you pray for someone to be healed, ask, "Is it ok if I lay hands on you?" (Permission is especially important with strangers.) Immediately have them test their condition before you say any sort of word of authority. See if they were healed simply by God's power touching them!

Supplemental Reading:
❑   Acts 10:38
❑   Luke 5:17
❑   Luke 8:46

DAY 24
THE PRESENCE OF GOD

Art Thomas

...A lot of times when people come into a church and the worship is going, well the presence of the Lord starts coming in...and He'll probably heal just about anybody that's not watching ...He likes to heal people, and I think they just kind of – by default – get into the presence of God; and then, all of a sudden, they find out that they're changed. Just like Moses was in the presence of God – he didn't even know he was glowing when he came back; but the people said, "Put something of your face!" You get into the presence of God and things happen to you physically. Now that's a physical manifestation: his skin glowed. And so I just think that the presence of God will do it.

~ Leonard Jones

Luke 5:17 — Now it happened on a certain day, as He was teaching, that there were Pharisees and teachers of the law sitting by, who had come out of every

town of Galilee, Judea, and Jerusalem.
And the power of the Lord was present to
heal them. (NKJV)

I was in a small Ugandan village called Isegero on a Sunday morning. The church was made of mud and sticks and had a grass roof. The people of the village filled the place that day to hear me speak, but that wasn't going to happen.

In the morning, the Holy Spirit told me not to preach but to simply invite His presence. This concept is awkward theologically because we know that God is always with us, so inviting Him to "come" seems to imply that He needs to move toward us from somewhere else. When my wife was pregnant with our first son, Josiah, we would say, "When the baby comes, we will do this or that." We talked about Joey as though he was coming later when the reality was that he was right there with us already inside of my wife. He was both present and coming and the same time. When we spoke of him "coming," what we really meant was that we would be able to see and interact with him—not merely know intellectually that he was with us.

The same is true of the Holy Spirit. On one hand, we know that He is everywhere at once—"omnipresent" to use a theological term. In fact, as believers, we know that He is within us at all times. And yet, at other times, we know that He will do a particular thing in a particular place that He is not doing in another place. These are the times when He comes out of hiding and we become aware of His presence in the natural realm.

That Sunday morning in Isegero, we invited the Holy Spirit to come, and then we waited in silence. After about five awkward minutes, something happened. Some of the people began to shake. Some of them were spontaneously healed. A few began to weep in repentance.

To make a long story short, every person at that meeting who needed to be healed was completely healed. The only "human" ministry came from a small group of children who started running around and laying hands on people until everyone was healed—and I'm not entirely sure that it was necessary. An old woman's paralyzed leg was healed. Eye problems, chest pain, headaches, and fevers ceased in the presence of God. Even a couple demons came out of people without anyone speaking a word of authority. God's presence did a tremendous work in that place with little help from me or any other minister. We simply agreed with what He wanted to do, and then we allowed Him to do whatever He pleased. God had an agenda, and all we had to do was let Him minister.

The more we talk about God's consistency and the fact that He never changes—the more we talk about Jesus being the same yesterday, today, and forever—the easier it becomes to treat God like a force rather than like a Person. Knowing that it is always God's will to heal can make us forget that there are times when He is particularly in the mood for healing.

Wanting to do something in general and wanting to do something specifically are two different things. Generally speaking, I always want to spend time with my wife, but I am often doing other things instead. If my wife interrupts those other things to visit with me, I'll typically drop what I'm doing and spend some time with her simply because that's what I always want to do anyway. But there are also times when I specifically want to be with my wife, and so I go spend time with her on my own initiative.

Similarly, God always wants to heal, so I can have confidence that whenever I minister healing, He will show up and do the work. But there are also times—as in today's scripture passage—when God shows up in power specifically because He wants to heal people; and in these moments, it sometimes feels like you're barely involved in the process.

Whenever I'm leading a healing ministry training at a church, I finish by having the people minister to each other. I have never had a meeting where people weren't healed during this time, so I know God always meets us with His healing power. But I have experienced a few cases when it seemed as though God's personality shined through, and He began healing people before we even had an opportunity to minister to anyone! In these cases, something in my spirit would recognize that God's power was present to heal, and before we even began to pray, I would ask everyone to test their conditions and see if anyone had already been healed. Usually laughter erupts from the congregation as looks of shock spread on the faces of several people who had stood for prayer. We then hear a handful of testimonies before praying for the rest and seeing even more miracles.

Never forget that God is a Person and that even though He is everywhere, and even though He is always willing to heal, there are times when He will exercise His Sovereign right to heal without our help—simply because He is God and He specifically wants to do so. We can't rely on these times (only choosing to minister when God shows up in power), but we do need to learn to recognize them and partner with God whenever He wants to do something specific in a given time and place.

Prayer Starter:

❑ Thank God for always wanting to heal people and for His willingness to partner with you at any time and in any place.

❑ Ask the Lord to help you to be aware of His desires so that you can humbly partner with Him when He wants to do something specific.

❑ Ask the Lord to show up in power when you minister to other people so that He can accomplish more than your own expectations.

Journal Experience:

While God is wildly more intricate and unfathomable than any human being, understanding our own human tendencies can help us avoid the problem of viewing God as a force rather than the Person that He is.

Make a list of three things you generally want to do that, if given the opportunity, you would drop everything to do them. Then make a list of three things that you will actually be doing today *because you want to*, regardless of someone else making the opportunity available.

Things I'd generally like to do if given the opportunity:

Things I specifically want and intend to do today:

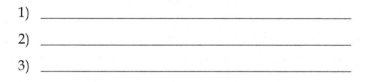

If someone were to approach you with an opportunity to do something you *generally* want to do, what would motivate you to do that thing? Would it be because you were manipulated into doing it? Or would it be because you were given an opportunity to do something you like? What does this imply to you about God's will and healing ministry?

_____

_____

_____

_____

_____

_____

_____

_____

_____

_____

_____

_____

_____

_____

_____

_____

_____

_____

_____

Action Step:

Ask the Lord if there's anything He specifically wants to do today in your sphere of influence. If you find yourself with a particular thought on your heart, look for the right opportunity to fulfill your role in the process. But even if nothing comes to mind, look for opportunities to do something God desires in general, and see Him meet you where you are.

Supplemental Reading:
❑ Psalm 16:11
❑ Psalm 139:7
❑ Psalm 97:5

DAY 25
UNUSUAL METHODS

Art Thomas

Sometimes we don't even have to lay hands on people. So it's not about you; it's about Him. He just chooses to use us because, you know that the Father has all the muscle — if you want to call it that — and He just makes us look good!

~ *Cynthia Beckley*

John 9:6-7 — After saying this, He spit on the ground, made some mud with the saliva, and put it on the man's eyes. "Go," He told him, "wash in the Pool of Siloam" (this word means "Sent"). So the man went and washed, and came home seeing. (NIV)

Acts 5:15 — As a result, people brought the sick into the streets and laid them on beds and mats so that at least Peter's shadow might fall on some of them as he passed by. (NIV)

> **Acts 19:11-12** — And God did unusual
> and extraordinary miracles by the hands
> of Paul, so that handkerchiefs or towels or
> aprons which had touched his skin were
> carried away and put upon the sick, and
> their diseases left them and the evil spirits
> came out of them. (AMP)

"You've got to hear what happened," said a grinning pastor at whose church I had conducted a healing ministry training the previous year. "My wife got this goiter on her neck that swelled up to about the size of half a baseball. Our church had been praying for her for weeks without seeing results. But then she and I were sitting on the couch, and I felt like the Holy Spirit told me to slap it! I didn't want a divorce, so I sheepishly said, 'Honey, I don't know what to tell you, but I feel like God's telling me to slap that thing.' She didn't say a word, threw her head back, and pointed at it. So then I slapped it, and it instantly disappeared!"

Stunned (and relieved that it worked), I joyfully chuckled out a reply: "That wasn't in my training!"

There are times when God brings healing in unusual ways — ways that do not involve the typical methods of laying hands on a person or speaking a word of authority.

A couple days ago, we talked about God ministering His power to people through physical contact from a believer. But when Peter was walking down the street in Acts 5, merely his shadow was healing people! And it wasn't that he had a solar-powered healing ministry — the Greek seems to imply that they simply needed to come into proximity to him (in other words, he could thankfully still heal on a cloudy day!). The presence of God was not trapped *within* Peter—God's Spirit was *upon* him, touching people who simply came too close.

In another case, cloth articles that had touched Paul's skin carried the same supercharged power as the cloth cloak Jesus wore that brought healing to many (Matthew 14:35-36 and Mark 6:56). These cloth articles—handkerchiefs, towels, or aprons—were brought to the sick, and the demons fled as though Jesus Himself had been standing there.

Throughout the New Testament, God's power seems to spread like spiritual electricity—"zapping" people and charging objects that came too close to a believer—the difference being that the Holy Spirit is a Person rather than a mere electric charge, so He doesn't "zap" by happenstance. He is very deliberate about partnering with human faith.

We also see unusual healings that I would suggest may be ministered through authority—like when Jesus put mud on the blind man's eyes and told him to wash it off in a certain pool, or like when Elisha told Naaman that his leprosy would be healed if he dipped seven times in the Jordan River (2 Kings 5), or like when my pastor friend slapped his wife's goiter.

You may remember that our authority in Christ flows from our relationship with our Father. Occasionally, God tells us to minister healing in a certain way that may seem strange—not because it's a medical prescription from heaven (mud doesn't open blind eyes, and slaps don't heal swollen thyroid glands) but because when we obey His instruction, we find ourselves submitting to His authority. Authority comes from obedience to our Father, so obedience produces results. It's not the unusual method that is powerful on its own; it's the obedience that brings us under the flow of God's authority.

Many people from our film have seen God heal in unusual ways. Dr. Karl Bandlien saw a man's dead leg revived when he simply washed it with saline water. Pete Cabrera Jr. once (in Jesus' name) commanded a plastic spoon to heal every person it touched, and then he started handing it to people and seeing them healed. Brook Potter told me a story of a man he knew who baked a cake and declared to a room of people, "Every person who eats this cake will be healed," and they all were. Sean Logue told me multiple stories of using the flashlight on his iPhone to cast a shadow on people, and they were healed. Leonard Jones played his violin to minister healing to a room full of people. And we filmed a student on the street in Redding, California, who was healed because one of the other Bethel School of Supernatural Ministry students handed him a picture they drew with crayons that loosely matched his basic description (shirt color, nearby grass) and his physical condition.

The only limit on what God will use to minister healing is the limit of love. As long as something can be done while conveying our Lord's pure and matchless love, He considers it an available option. Some of these methods work because our obedience brings us under the flow of His authority. Other methods work because God's power is transferred from one person to another through unusual means. In all cases, God is the One who does the work, and we are the vessels whom He uses.

A study of the Gospels and the book of Acts will show that unusual methods of healing seem to be the exception rather than the rule. If we're not careful, we can become more enamored with the methods we use than we are with the voice of the Lord. And when this happens, we find ourselves quickly slipping outside of His authority.

Here's what obedience looks like: (1) Follow the revealed commission of Jesus (speaking with authority and laying hands) whenever you have no instruction, (2) be creative when you feel that He is giving you that liberty, and (3) follow His instructions to the letter whenever He gives a specific direction.

Remember your role as His son—remember your place on Jesus' throne and the very real power you carry from the Holy Spirit. Practice learning to hear God's voice. And above all, don't be afraid to try new things in healing ministry as you seek to obey the Lord.

(And as a general rule, I don't recommend slapping anything!)

Prayer Starter:

- ❏ Thank the Lord for His creativity and His desire to heal people in any way possible.
- ❏ Ask the Holy Spirit to teach you to perceive what God is saying or instructing when you minister healing so that you can be obedient to the Lord's instructions.

❑ Ask God to help you to walk in the humility of Jesus as you minister to other people in unusual ways—unashamed to obey God no matter how strange you may look.

Journal Experience:

I was once at a meeting in Brooklyn, New York, when the Holy Spirit told me to minister to hearing loss before I preached the sermon. Imagine yourself in my shoes. Part of me was intimidated because if it didn't work, then I was going to have an interesting time teaching the congregation to minister healing after that! But another part of me had seen God come through so many times before that I knew it would work. Not to mention, hearing God's voice produces faith, so I had that working in my favor (Romans 10:17).

What would be the most intimidating concern in your mind if God asked you to do something unusual in front of others to minister healing? How would you convince yourself to try it anyway?

_____

_____

_____

_____

_____

_____

_____

Action Step:

Cynthia Beckley mentioned in our film about ministering healing over the online video-conferencing service, Skype. I too have used Skype to minister healing. I've seen people healed through Facebook and e-mail too.

Today, use some sort of media to minister healing to someone. This could be electronic media (as in the previous examples) or physical media (like writing a note, drawing a picture, baking a cake, etc.). Simply ask the Lord to instruct you what method to use, and then follow through on what He tells you. If you don't hear anything in reply, be creative. See what happens!

Supplemental Reading:
❑ John 14:12
❑ John 20:30
❑ John 21:25

SECTION 6:
Attaching the Message to the Ministry

DAY 26
CAPTURING ATTENTION

Art Thomas

---

*I have not prayed with one person that I can remember —
that was healed – that did not receive Jesus Christ (that
didn't know Him). They were always hungry to receive
the One that touched them.*

~ *Michel Borchardt*

Matthew 15:29-31 — Jesus left there and
went along the Sea of Galilee. Then He
went up on a mountainside and sat
down. Great crowds came to Him,
bringing the lame, the blind, the crippled,
the mute and many others, and laid
them at His feet; and He healed them.
The people were amazed when they saw
the mute speaking, the crippled made
well, the lame walking and the blind
seeing. And they praised the God of
Israel. (NIV)

Sometimes the miraculous can draw a crowd and make them aware of the reality of God. Other times, God will display His wonders to incite the curiosity of an individual. In either case, God's power can capture the attention of people who would have otherwise continued going about their ordinary lives.

One of my favorite clips from the film came from Thomas Fischer as he was training another man to minister healing and share the Gospel on the street. One young man's back was healed, and then the other's detached kneecap was healed. As the two young men were still trying to mentally and emotionally process what just happened to them, Tom immediately shifted gears into a presentation of the Gospel.

If you're one who pays attention to detail, you may have noticed the second young man subtly reach for the cigarette that his cousin was holding for him but then wave it away as he realized he didn't even care about it in that moment. The two young men listened intently to Tom's words. In the full-length video, their conversation lasted several minutes, and the young men even had questions for Tom. The miracles that happened to them had awakened spiritual hunger, and Tom had a captive audience for the Good News about Jesus.

In Psalm 34:8, we are reminded to "taste and see that the Lord is good." Many people in this world have formed false opinions about God based on disappointments, psychological wounds, and unbelief. But if we can give them a taste of the Lord's goodness, they're going to need to process their new personal experience in contrast to their opinions.

When we argue theology with the lost, we rarely achieve anything of value. Theology may be the study of a God who is love, but theology itself is not love. In the words of missionary Heidi Baker, "Love looks like something." If you merely talk *about* God, people may compare your verbalized thoughts to their own life experiences, see a complete absence of personal encounters with the God you claim exists, and then ignore what you have to say. But if you introduce that person to the God who loves them — if you show them love in practical, tangible ways (including, but not limited to healing ministry) — then you have a situation of far greater value: a person trying to reconcile their personal history with the God they just encountered.

Prayer Starter:

- ❑ Thank the Father for loving the world so much that He joyfully and willingly reveals Himself to those who don't know Him, allowing them to experience His goodness in tangible ways.
- ❑ Ask the Lord to deal with any fears in your heart that might cause you to miss an opportunity to explain the Gospel after ministering healing to someone who doesn't know Him.
- ❑ Ask the Lord to bring people across your path who need both physical healing and spiritual salvation. Ask Him to give you discernment, along with the right words and actions, to introduce the person to Jesus in a meaningful way.

Journal Experience:

How did God capture your attention and bring you to salvation?

_____

_____

_____

_____

_____

_____

_____

_____

_____

_____

_____

_____

_____

_____

_____

_____

_____

_____

_____

Action Step:

The next time you minister healing, ask the person if they have ever met the Jesus who just healed them. Ask if they want to know Him more. See where the conversation goes, and trust the Holy Spirit to direct you.

Supplemental Reading:
❑   Psalm 34
❑   Acts 8:4-8

DAY 27
PROVING THE POWER OF JESUS TO SAVE

James Loruss

Just preaching the Gospel without God's power behind – it does not bring joy. Speaking about Jesus, but without showing the power of Jesus, you are meaning nothing to people. ...Because He gives eternal life and He gives also life physically. When people are healed, you see them dancing – you see them even preaching to other people about the goodness of Christ.

~ *Paul Basuule Habib*

> **James 5:15** — And the prayer of faith will save the sick, and the Lord will raise him up. And if he has committed sins, he will be forgiven. (NKJV)

Whenever I see someone healed, I like to tell them that the same price Jesus paid for their physical body was the same blood poured out for their forgiveness. I've had times when someone was healed and they stood there as if nothing happened; but then I tell them, "You know, the same thing Jesus just did to that pain in your body, He did to your sins. God says you are forgiven, and He's pursuing your heart right now."

You wouldn't believe the impact this has! People need to know that they're forgiven. What good is it for someone to walk away healed without being introduced to the Healer? I'm not saying that every person you minister to has to pray a prayer of salvation right there. I'm simply saying we must always keep this message of healing attached to the power of Jesus to save.

Healing ministry is another way for God's heart of reconciliation to flow out of you. Second Corinthians 5:17-19 says, "Therefore, if anyone is in Christ, the new creation has come: The old has gone, the new is here! All this is from God, who reconciled us to himself through Christ and gave us the ministry of reconciliation: that God was reconciling the world to himself in Christ, not counting people's sins against them. And he has committed to us the message of reconciliation". You have an incredible responsibility: God has entrusted you with both His Spirit and His message. You were given the message of reconciliation. In the words of Reece Hale, "I don't want to just watch somebody who was limping get healed and then walk straight into hell. Woe to me if I do that because I have the words of life living inside of me — that I get to share — and it's free! And it's my joy to give it away."

Healing ministry proves that the blood of Jesus still has power. And if His blood has power to save your body, then His blood has power to save your spirit. Whenever you point this out to a person who was just healed, you are giving them an opportunity to put their faith in the One who loves them more than they could ever imagine.

Prayer Starter:

❏ Thank God for reconciling you to Himself through the blood of Jesus.
❏ Thank Jesus for making you clean through His blood.
❏ Ask the Holy Spirit to minister through you the power of Jesus to save—not just bringing His healing power, but leading people to Him for their full salvation.

Journal Experience:

Knowing what you now know, why do you suppose God chooses to use Christians to minister healing rather than simply eliminating sickness and disease from the world?

_____

_____

_____

_____

_____

_____

_____

_____

_____

_____

_____

_____

_____

_____

_____

_____

_____

Action Step:

The entire point of using healing ministry to prove the power of Jesus to save is that a person is not merely hearing someone else's experience with God, but they are hearing an explanation of their own experience. Nevertheless, testimonies are an awesome way to quicken someone's mind to what God is capable of doing. In fact, testimonies seem to carry with them a certain measure of spiritual momentum toward a new miracle, implying that if God could do it before, He can do it now (like when David recounted the testimonies of God helping him kill a lion and a bear before he approached Goliath).

At this point in our devotional study, you should have a handful of testimonies about God healing people (even if it's just testimonies from what you saw in the movie). Today, share one of those testimonies with someone else.

Supplemental Reading:
❑   Ephesians 1:7

DAY 28
REVEALING THE HEART OF THE FATHER

James Loruss (with Art Thomas)

Jesus leads people to the Father. Everything Jesus did pointed to the heart of the Father for humanity.
~ Daniel Phillips

John 14:6-11 — Jesus answered, "I am the way and the truth and the life. No one comes to the Father except through me. If you really know me, you will know my Father as well. From now on, you do know him and have seen him."

Philip said, "Lord, show us the Father and that will be enough for us."

Jesus answered: "Don't you know me, Philip, even after I have been among you such a long time? Anyone who has seen me has seen the Father. How can you say, 'Show us the Father'? Don't you believe that I am in the Father, and that the Father is in me? The words I say to you I do not speak on my own authority.

> Rather, it is the Father, living in me, who is
> doing his work. Believe me when I say that
> I am in the Father and the Father is in me;
> or at least believe on the evidence of the
> works themselves. (NIV)

Jesus is the perfect representation of our Father in heaven. Jesus didn't make a move without His Father because they are one — one in purpose, one in nature, one in mission, and so forth. If you saw Jesus, you saw the Father.

Jesus is the mediator between God and men (1 Timothy 2:5), but sometimes we take this thought too far. I've heard some people talk about God the Father as though He's some muscle-bound aggressor being held back by Jesus, saying, "Let it go, man! Just walk away." It sounds ridiculous when we put it in those terms, but how many times do we think like that? We assume God wants to destroy us, but, thankfully, we have Jesus protecting us.

That's absurd!

God the Father is revealed through Jesus. Hebrews 1:3 calls Jesus "the exact representation of [the Father's] being." If you believe something to be true about the Father that you cannot reconcile with the example Jesus Christ demonstrated in the Bible, then you have reason to revisit why you believe what you believe. God is not double-minded. Jesus isn't the sweet, forgiving counterpart to a sadistic destroyer. Jesus and the Father are one.

We praise Jesus for making the ultimate sacrifice (and He did!), but what about the Father? Didn't He give up His only Son? That was "His baby" — perfect and precious in every way. He must love you and me a whole lot if saving us was worth sacrificing Jesus. Dan Mohler puts it this way: "The 'I love you' from God is Jesus on the cross."

The heart of the Father has not changed from the beginning of time. Since the fall of man—beginning with Adam—God has been pursuing us. In Genesis 3, Adam and Eve had just eaten the forbidden fruit and were hiding from God. What did God do? It says in verse 9, "But the Lord God called to the man, 'Where are you?'" God was running for Adam—not for vengeance, but for relationship.

God has always pursued humanity. His heart from the beginning was always relationship. His plan from the beginning was always Jesus (Revelation 13:8).

Then, in verse 21, we see that God makes garments of skin for Adam and Eve. Where do you think this skin came from? It came from the sacrifice of an animal—a foreshadowing of God's sacrificial heart and His desire to cover the sin of His children.

Jesus perfectly represented the Father, and He healed every single person who came to Him. He never said, "I'm sorry, but My Father is building character in you, so you'll have to stay crippled." He never said, "My Father's answer is 'not yet,' so ask Me to lay hands on you the next time I visit your town." Jesus always healed, and He always healed right away. That's because it was what the Father wanted!

And if our Father doesn't change (James 1:17), and if Jesus doesn't change (Hebrews 13:8), why would we expect His will to be any different today? The heart of the Father is always to save, always to set free, and always to heal. Not all are saved, not all are delivered, and not all are healed—but these things are not expressions of the heart of God; and that's why you can't find them in the life or ministry of Jesus.

Yes, God is allowed to say "no" or "not yet" — after all, He's God! But isn't it interesting that Jesus never exercised that option? Instead, He revealed a Father whose will was always "yes" and "now." Perhaps God is more willing to heal than we are to believe. God doesn't need to change — we do.

Healing ministry is in the heart of the Father. As Cynthia Beckley said in the film, "The first [descriptive] name of God in the Bible is Jehovah Rapha, and it means 'the God that heals.' Right from the very beginning, that was God's heart for His people. He wanted us to know that He's not just 'Father,' He's not just 'God,' but He heals people."

Just as Jesus revealed the Father, we are sent to reveal Jesus. It's our mission. Just as Jesus is one with the Father, Paul says that when we have been united with Jesus, we are one with Him (1 Corinthians 6:17). Healing ministry reveals the compassion of God all by itself, but God wants to be seen in more than a mere miracle — He wants to be seen through our entire lives. We each have a responsibility to be conformed into the likeness of Jesus (Romans 8:29). As you minister healing, consider how your accompanying words, attitudes, and actions reveal the heart of the Father. Learn to walk in unity with Jesus so that people can experience God in a greater measure as you minister healing to them. "And whatever you do, whether in word or deed, do it all in the name of the Lord Jesus, giving thanks to God the Father through Him" (Colossians 3:17).

Prayer Starter:

❏ Thank Father God for His sacrifice of His only Son on your behalf.
❏ Ask the Holy Spirit to help you to align your own heart and motivation with that of the Father through Christ.
❏ Ask God to help you reveal His heart to those around you.

Journal Experience:

How is the heart of God being revealed through your life? Write down three ways that you can show God's heart to someone today.

_____

_____

_____

_____

_____

_____

_____

_____

_____

_____

_____

_____

_____

_____

_____

_____

_____

_____

_____

Action Step:

Choose one or more of the three things you wrote down in your Journal Experience, and carry it out today.

Supplemental Reading:
- ❑ John 5:19-30
- ❑ John 6:38
- ❑ John 7:16-18
- ❑ John 8:28-29
- ❑ John 15:1-9
- ❑ 1 Timothy 2:5-6
- ❑ Hebrews 1:3

DAY 29
PROCLAIMING THE DOMINION OF JESUS

Art Thomas (with Jonathan Ammon)

Somebody said to me a while back, "Preacher, that's hypnotism." ...I know hypnotists who would give their bottom dollar to be able to hypnotize the blind and have them see — the deaf and have them hear — the lame and have them walk... If it's hypnotism, I'll hypnotize the first one; you get the next one, and let's see you do it... Somebody has challenged me often times — offering as much as a $2,500 reward — for one person I've healed. I'll tell you what I'll do with those "somebodies" — I'll let them sit in with me in the healing line, I'll let them pray for everybody just before I do. I'd like to have them make the eyes of the blind see. I'll let them pray for those that are on crutches and make them walk. I'll let them pray for those that have cancers so when they feel for them, they can't find them. Brother, they'll pray first; and after they're done praying, I'll show them what the God of heaven can do with the same person after they prayed for them.

~ Jack Coe, Sr.
from the message "Divine Healing on Trial"

> **Luke 10:19** — I have given you authority
> to trample on snakes and scorpions and
> to overcome all the power of the enemy;
> nothing will harm you. (NIV)

I found myself standing on a makeshift stage in front of 250 Ugandan spectators in a rural Muslim village overrun with witchdoctors. Visions were running through my mind of me — beaten and bleeding — trying to dig my way out of a little shed in the middle of the night.

Pastor Paul Basuule Habib (who you met in the movie) had arranged this meeting for the purpose of planting a new church in this village; and since I was living with him during that half of October 2011, he thought it would be great to have me preach to the villagers.

I read a passage from Jesus' "Sermon on the Mount" that we call "the Beatitudes." At the end of His list of blessings, our Lord says, "Blessed are those who are persecuted because of righteousness, for theirs is the kingdom of heaven" (Matthew 5:10). When I reached the verse about persecution, I paused. I realized that these people would very likely face real persecution for the message I was bringing. I knew that when I left, people might be beaten, kicked from their homes, and possibly even murdered for receiving the message of the Gospel. These people needed to know that Jesus is alive and that He is supreme. And the potential persecutors (especially the witchdoctors and Muslim imams) needed to know the power of the Jesus they would be persecuting.

I said, "You know, the people who persecute Christians are cowards because they fear gods that have no power. In fact, if you are a witchdoctor or an imam, I want you to come up here on this stage with me. Bring your biggest demon. Bring your Muslim god. I'll prove to you that they have no power. Jesus Christ is King. He has *all* power!"

And then I waited.

Our King is the King of all Kings. His authority extends over every authority, and He has commissioned us to exert that authority over every demonic force and power. Every rebel must be struck down and cast out in Jesus' name until the last day when the devil and his servants will be thrown into eternal punishment.

The world lies under the power of the wicked one (1 John 5:19), but God has trusted us with an authority and kingdom to spread over the entire earth. The kingdom of God banishes every sickness, every disease, every demon, and every physical infirmity. When the sick are healed, Christ's rule and dominion has been enforced and established. Jesus said, "heal the sick there, and say to them, the kingdom of God has come near to you" (Luke 10:9). We are commissioned to proclaim the rule, reign, and dominion of the highest authority: Jesus Christ.

It was a long thirty seconds that I waited, but no one came to the stage.

"You see?" I prodded, "They *are* cowards! They know that what I say is true! And to prove it to all of you, if you have a sickness or a disease—eye problems, ear problems, crippled legs, pain in your body, or anything else—if you are able, I want you to place your hand where the problem is right now. In Jesus' name, I command every sickness to leave now…" I commanded the blind eyes and deaf ears to open. I commanded cripples to walk. I basically spoke to everything that came to my mind and made sure the people knew I was doing it on Jesus' behalf.

And then came the moment of truth. I continued, "Now try to do something you couldn't do. Move around. If you are now completely healed, I want you to raise your hand and wave it."

Across the field of 250 people, about 40 hands waved boldly in the air. From there I continued to preach from Colossians 1 about the supremacy of Christ. I contradicted the teachings of Islam by proclaiming that Jesus is the Son of God and that He did indeed die and raise again. And at the end, 50 people came to salvation.

That day, we planted a church.

Prayer Starter:

- ❑ Praise and worship Jesus as the King of Kings and Lord of Lords. Declare His ultimate rule and authority. Thank Him for being such a powerful and kind Ruler.
- ❑ Ask the Lord to extend His dominion within you and touch each part of your heart and life. Declare His authority over every part of your life. Ask Him to rule your life completely and identify any part of your life that is out of order.
- ❑ Ask the Lord to use you to extend His kingdom and rule of love over the entire earth. Ask Him to give you marching orders. Ask Him how you can extend His kingdom in your community.

Journal Experience:

Write down everything from the kingdom of darkness that intimidates you. This may be people from certain false religions, specific fears, particular sicknesses, diseases, people or governments, or anything else that causes you to hesitate in taking bold action for Jesus Christ. For each item you write down, strike a line through it, and then write next to it, "Jesus is bigger."

_____

_____

_____

_____

_____

_____

_____

_____

_____

_____

_____

_____

_____

_____

_____

Action Step:

Read Luke 10:1-9. Jesus instructs His laborers, "Whatever city you enter, and they receive you, eat such things as are set before you. And *heal the sick there*, and say to them, 'The kingdom of God has come near to you.'" Think about the sick people in your town or city. The next time you see someone healed in your city, tell them, "The Kingdom of God has come near to you." Explain what that means. Today, ask someone, "What does 'The Kingdom of God has come near to you' mean to you?"

Supplemental Reading:
- ❑ 1 Kings 18:16-46
- ❑ Luke 11:14-26
- ❑ Luke 13:10-17
- ❑ 2 Corinthians 10:3-4

DAY 30
DECLARING GOD'S FORGIVENESS

James Loruss (with Art Thomas)

It says He bore our sickness and disease on the cross – the same cross [where] He bore our sin.

~ *Daniel Phillips*

Mark 2:3-12 — Some men came, bringing to him a paralyzed man, carried by four of them. Since they could not get him to Jesus because of the crowd, they made an opening in the roof above Jesus by digging through it and then lowered the mat the man was lying on. When Jesus saw their faith, he said to the paralyzed man, "Son, your sins are forgiven."

Now some teachers of the law were sitting there, thinking to themselves, "Why does this fellow talk like that? He's blaspheming! Who can forgive sins but God alone?"

Immediately Jesus knew in his spirit

that this was what they were thinking in their hearts, and he said to them, "Why are you thinking these things? Which is easier: to say to this paralyzed man, 'Your sins are forgiven,' or to say, 'Get up, take your mat and walk'? But I want you to know that the Son of Man has authority on earth to forgive sins." So he said to the man, "I tell you, get up, take your mat and go home." He got up, took his mat and walked out in full view of them all. This amazed everyone and they praised God, saying, "We have never seen anything like this!" (NIV)

Jesus was proving a point here. He was showing that the power to heal the sick is the same power that forgives sins.

Jesus is amazing! Do you realize He not only paid the price for you to be completely free, but you now have the honor and privilege of extending that same forgiveness to those around you? Healing ministry should never be separated from the love and forgiveness God offers.

James 5:15 says, "And the prayer offered in faith will make the sick person well; the Lord will raise them up. If they have sinned, they will be forgiven." The implication here seems to be that forgiveness comes as part of the package when a person is healed. When you minister healing to the sick, you can rightly say, "This is proof that God has forgiven you of all your sin! The same blood of Jesus that just healed you also paid the price for every sin you've ever committed!"

Strangely, in the very next verse, James reverses the order, saying, "Therefore confess your sins to each other and pray for each other so that you may be healed." In one case, healing comes first and forgiveness happens automatically; in the other case, forgiveness is first and healing comes second. Which one is it?

Art always likes to say, "The blood of Jesus is messy; you get a little bit on you for one thing, and it tends to get all over everything." We like to categorize everything—Jesus' blood paid for my sins and His body was beaten for my healing. While this may be true, I like to simplify things: Jesus poured out His own life for my complete restoration before God. Jesus paid for our complete wholeness—body, soul and spirit.

You are called to not only heal the sick, but to offer forgiveness as well. Jesus instructed His disciples to proclaim the forgiveness of God to people so that they could be forgiven (John 20:23). Healing and forgiveness should not be separated. I've found that forgiveness is not just a choice I make but also a lifestyle that I live. Everyone I encounter has been extended that forgiveness—Jesus already paid for their sins (1 John 2:2). My role is to do what Jesus did for the paralyzed man: "Son, your sins are forgiven."

Many Christians struggle with this idea of extending forgiveness before a person surrenders his or her life to Jesus. Realize that there is a difference between forgiveness and reconciliation. Forgiveness is simply a decision to stop wishing disaster on a person and to instead love them through self-sacrificial kindness. Reconciliation, on the other hand, is a restoration of relationship. When one party forgives the other, the result is not necessarily reconciliation. That would require the decision of both parties. However, it does make reconciliation possible.

Jesus instructed us to love ("self-sacrifice for") our enemies; and in this way, we exemplify our Father in heaven who loved the world so much that He gave His only Son. "While we were still sinners, Christ died for us" (Romans 5:8). You can rightly say to the worst sinner, "Your sins are forgiven" and be absolutely right. And if that person will believe and receive your message, they will be reconciled to God.

When the sinful woman poured perfume on the feet of Jesus, wet His feet with her tears, and wiped them with her hair, the reason was that she recognized the reality of God's forgiveness. In Luke 7:47, Jesus spoke in the past-tense, saying, "Therefore, I tell you, her many sins have been forgiven — as her great love has shown. But whoever has been forgiven little loves little." Her act of worship was inspired by the fact that she had already been forgiven; but in the next verse, Jesus solidified this reality, ministering to the woman's heart by verbalizing God's forgiveness: "Your sins are forgiven" (Luke 7:48).

Minister healing to everyone, regardless of their religions or the stubbornness of their hearts. In the same way, proclaim God's forgiveness to everyone, no matter how much they may hate God or live as though He doesn't exist. Then plead as Paul did for their salvation: "We implore you on Christ's behalf: Be reconciled to God!" (2 Corinthians 5:20.)

Prayer Starter:

❑ Praise God for His grace and forgiveness that was extended to you when you least deserved it.

❑ Take a moment to meditate on the completeness of God's forgiveness toward you, and allow thankfulness to rise up in your heart.

❑ Pray for three people you know who do not yet know God's forgiveness. Ask God to open doors for them to experience His goodness, and ask Him to give you an opportunity to show His love to them.

Journal Experience:

Write a short testimony of a time you chose to forgive someone. What did they do that hurt you? Why did you choose to forgive them? Did you feel like forgiving or was it difficult? What happened in your own heart after you forgave? Did reconciliation also happen?

Action Step:

Ask the Lord if there's anyone in your life who needs to know that He has already forgiven them. Somehow contact them today and tell them that "God wants you to know that He has forgiven everything you've ever done wrong, and He wants to have a relationship with you."

Supplemental Reading:
- Matthew 6:14-15
- Luke 7:36-50
- 2 Corinthians 5:11-21

SECTION 7:
Healing Ministry as a Normal Part of Life

DAY 31
MINISTERING TO FAMILY

Art Thomas

I've lost family…two cousins and an uncle. And I don't know why — sometimes because we're so intimate with family, that sometimes gets in the way somehow (our love and compassion for them). I can't explain why that is, but that has been probably the biggest hurdle of sorts [for me]. But, you know, you trust God, and you push through it.

~ *Brook Potter*

John 11:17-44 — On his arrival, Jesus found that Lazarus had already been in the tomb for four days. Now Bethany was less than two miles from Jerusalem, and many Jews had come to Martha and Mary to comfort them in the loss of their brother. When Martha heard that Jesus was coming, she went out to meet him, but Mary stayed at home.

"Lord," Martha said to Jesus, "if you had been here, my brother would not have died. But I know that even now God will give you whatever you ask."

Jesus said to her, "Your brother will rise again."

Martha answered, "I know he will rise again in the resurrection at the last day."

Jesus said to her, "I am the resurrection and the life. The one who believes in me will live, even though they die; and whoever lives by believing in me will never die. Do you believe this?"

"Yes, Lord," she replied, "I believe that you are the Messiah, the Son of God, who is to come into the world."

After she had said this, she went back and called her sister Mary aside. "The Teacher is here," she said, "and is asking for you." When Mary heard this, she got up quickly and went to him. Now Jesus had not yet entered the village, but was still at the place where Martha had met him. When the Jews who had been with Mary in the house, comforting her, noticed how quickly she got up and went out, they followed her, supposing she was going to the tomb to mourn there.

When Mary reached the place where Jesus was and saw him, she fell at his feet and said, "Lord, if you had been here, my brother would not have died."

When Jesus saw her weeping, and the Jews who had come along with her also weeping, he was deeply moved in spirit and troubled. "Where have you laid him?" he asked.

"Come and see, Lord," they replied.

Jesus wept.

Then the Jews said, "See how he loved him!"

But some of them said, "Could not he

who opened the eyes of the blind man have kept this man from dying?"

Jesus, once more deeply moved, came to the tomb. It was a cave with a stone laid across the entrance. "Take away the stone," he said.

"But, Lord," said Martha, the sister of the dead man, "by this time there is a bad odor, for he has been there four days."

Then Jesus said, "Did I not tell you that if you believe, you will see the glory of God?"

So they took away the stone. Then Jesus looked up and said, "Father, I thank you that you have heard me. I knew that you always hear me, but I said this for the benefit of the people standing here, that they may believe that you sent me."

When he had said this, Jesus called in a loud voice, "Lazarus, come out!" The dead man came out, his hands and feet wrapped with strips of linen, and a cloth around his face.

Jesus said to them, "Take off the grave clothes and let him go." (NIV)

The closer you are to a person, the easier it can sometimes be for faith to be affected by a sea of emotions. In this story, we have three examples of people who were close to Lazarus: Martha and Mary (who were sisters to Lazarus) and Jesus (who was not related by blood but did deeply love this family, as seen in John 11:5). Each person handled the situation differently.

First we see Martha. Her theology was great! She knew that Jesus was the Son of God. She was certain that even though Lazarus was dead, the Father would still give Jesus whatever He asked. But when Jesus promised that her brother would rise again, Martha struggled to see it happening in that moment and instead looked forward to the resurrection. Even after seeming to agree (by proclaiming that Jesus was the Messiah), Martha was the first person to object to rolling away the stone.

Second, we see Mary. She was incredibly distraught over her loss and even expressed frustration with Jesus, saying that if He had been there, Lazarus wouldn't have died. In Mary's mind, all hope was lost. Jesus didn't come through before, and she certainly wasn't expecting anything now.

Third, we see Jesus. He was deeply moved by the scene of mourning — so moved that He too began to weep. Some of the onlookers mocked Him, pointing out that His miraculous powers seemed to work for everyone else except His good friend. But Jesus was not swayed by the opinions of men or the lack of faith around Him. Instead, He looked to His Father and declared, "I thank You that You have heard Me. And I know that You always hear Me..." (NKJV). Jesus had more than the theology of Martha, and He had more than the emotion of Mary. Jesus had His identity firmly anchored in His sonship, His certainty about the Father's will, and His certainty that His Father loved and heard Him.

One of the most valuable things to notice here, though, is that Jesus did not rebuke Mary or Martha for a lack of faith. Just as He didn't blame the epileptic boy's father when His disciples couldn't cast a demon out, Jesus now met this family with the same mercy and grace. It is entirely possible for family to minister healing to each other (my wife and

I do it all the time); but there are times when our closeness to the person can overwhelm our emotions, and in these times, God completely understands our situation.

When you have the opportunity to minister healing to a family member, step one is to simply do it like you would for anyone else. The same hope and expectation you have for a complete stranger to be healed can be held as you minister to your family. Generally speaking, that's all you need to know! Jesus loved Lazarus deeply and He was overcome with emotion, but He was still able to minister resurrection life.

But in those cases where you recognize that you're either like Mary (distraught with emotion and questioning God) or like Martha (full of great theology but struggling to be certain that God will do a miracle at this moment), the best thing to do is find someone who is perhaps a little less emotionally invested in your loved one's life. There's absolutely nothing wrong with this, and Jesus never corrected such actions. Rather, the Bible is clear that there are times when one of us is weak, and the rest of the Church is to rally around us to address our struggle on our behalf (Romans 15:1). And in these times, our responsibility is simply to continue to care for the sick (as you saw in the lesson on Day 15).

When ministering to family, try to separate from your connection to the person within your earthly family tree and simply focus on your heavenly family tree (which is really just a "family stick": God the Father and you). In that moment, you are a son of God who speaks on behalf of Jesus— you're not a grieving husband, mother, aunt, cousin, brother, daughter, or nephew. Remember who you are, remember who Jesus is, and persevere in healing ministry. But don't be afraid to recognize and admit if your faith is wavering—it's normal, it's acceptable, and it opens a door for others to bear you up in your weakness. The responsibility for healing ministry belongs to the whole Church, and you don't have to carry that weight on your own.

Prayer Starter:

❑ Thank Jesus for setting an example that proved healing ministry can still happen in the midst of deep emotion and even grief. Thank the Father for always hearing you.

❑ Ask the Holy Spirit—the Spirit of sonship—to quicken your heart to the reality of your intimate relationship with Father God.

❑ Ask the Lord to help you remain grounded in your new "family tree" with the Father so that problems in your earthly family tree do not shake your faith. Ask Him to help you to bear others up when their faith for a loved one's healing is struggling.

Journal Experience:

What do you consider to be the most difficult aspect of ministering healing to a family member? Ask Jesus how to overcome that issue, and write down what comes to mind.

Action Step:

Choose one of the following three options: (1) Minister healing to a family member. (2) Admit to a fellow Christian that you're struggling in your faith for a family member's healing, and ask them to minister healing instead. (3) Find a friend who has a family member who needs healing, and minister to that friend's family member either at a distance or in person.

Supplemental Reading:
❏ Mark 1:29-31
❏ Romans 15:1-2

DAY 32
MINISTERING TO FRIENDS

Art Thomas

I've had that question asked so many times with Christians, and it's always from a Christian. They ask, "What happens if you pray for someone and they don't get healed? Do people get offended?" I say, "No! They think I'm crazy to begin with!" And when they don't, but then they see that I really care and love them...Jesus just comes through. And that's greater than any healing – when they see the real love of a real God who created everything.

~ Sean Logue

Mark 6:1-5a — Jesus left there and went to his hometown, accompanied by his disciples. When the Sabbath came, he began to teach in the synagogue, and many who heard him were amazed.

"Where did this man get these things?" they asked. "What's this wisdom that has been given him? What are these remarkable miracles he is performing?

> Isn't this the carpenter? Isn't this Mary's son
> and the brother of James, Joseph, Judas
> and Simon? Aren't his sisters here with us?"
> And they took offense at him.
>
> Jesus said to them, "A prophet is not
> without honor except in his own town,
> among his relatives and in his own
> home." He could not do any miracles
> there, except lay his hands on a few sick
> people and heal them. He was amazed
> at their lack of faith. (NIV)

Sometimes, the more familiar a person is with you, the more difficult it is for them to see you as someone who actually has something to offer them from God. This isn't as true among believers who have learned to value the presence of God in one another and learn from each other, but it's certainly common among those who view people from a worldly perspective.

When Jesus visited His hometown, the people took offense at Him (Matthew 13:57). "Isn't this Mary's son?" they asked. The people could only see Jesus' earthly identity and refused to believe that the little kid who used to run around their village could possibly have anything Messianic to offer.

Many people interpret this passage as though the unbelief of the people was somehow a force that was more powerful than Jesus' faith. If that's true, then it's the only time the unbelief of others managed to stop Him. After all, Jesus didn't have any trouble raising Lazarus from the dead (John 11:17-44). He once walked into the middle of a funeral procession and raised a dead boy (Luke 7:11-17). And when the disciples lacked the faith to cast a demon out of an epileptic boy, Jesus pointed to the entire generation — in other words, all the people around Him — as being "unbelieving and perverse" (Matthew 17:17); yet He still healed the boy (Matthew 17:14-20).

I have seen many people healed who didn't really believe for themselves. As a matter of fact, if unbelief were a force that stopped healing, then we wouldn't accomplish much of anything on the streets! Some of us have more faith in the power of someone's unbelief than we have faith in God!

But the problem in Jesus' hometown wasn't actually "unbelief." It was a "lack of faith" (Mark 6:6). There's a big difference (See Appendix C). Faith is a relational word whereas belief is an intellectual word. One refers to our trust in a person while the other refers to our embracing of information. If my wife says she will meet me in one location, but I believe she will be in another, then I have belief, but I don't have faith. And if I follow my belief rather than putting faith in my wife's words, then I'm not going to find her in the other place! Faith cannot happen apart from believing a person, but belief can happen apart from faith.

Whenever Jesus marveled at someone's faith, it wasn't necessarily their perfect faith in God (or else they could have been healed without approaching Him); rather, it always seemed to be their unwavering trust that Jesus (who they thought was merely a teacher or prophet, not yet understanding His divinity) would consistently minister healing on God's behalf. It wasn't a matter of believing the right information about God; it was a matter of trusting the Person of Jesus. When Jesus showed up in His hometown, the people had no expectation that God would use Him to do anything spectacular. They didn't trust Him to be the Messiah that He was. As far as they were concerned, Jesus wasn't good at anything except carpentry. It's far more likely that these people didn't come to Him for healing than that their lack of faith was somehow a power more potent than Jesus' faith.

In fact, in Luke's account (4:14-30), a very different picture is painted in which Jesus offended the people of His hometown with His preaching and pointed out that prophets are without honor in such situations. The crowd then chased Him away and tried to throw Him off a cliff! That didn't leave much of an opportunity for healing ministry!

Can you imagine one of the people from this crazed mob coming to Jesus and asking Him to heal them? And even if you could imagine such a thing, can you imagine Him riling up the crowd and saying, "It's not working, guys! Come on! You need to have more faith!"? Darkness is not a force; it's an absence of light. I've never seen a light bulb struggle because the darkness was too strong. In the same way, "lack of faith" is not a force. Faith is.

When ministering healing to friends, you'll occasionally encounter people who don't believe you have anything to offer them. But I've found that most people these days will at least give you an opportunity to try. Many will try to escape (or give you an out) rather than allowing you to persevere. I have learned to honor these requests, but not without at least explaining my desire to persevere and see them made whole "because Jesus wants it and already paid for it."

I have seen many of my friends healed — many of them from my home church. It is entirely possible to minister healing to friends. Even Jesus was able to heal "a few sick people" in His troublesome hometown (Mark 6:5). But don't allow yourself to be offended in the times when people you care about reject your offer to minister (or if they try to throw you off a cliff). Continue to love them and be their friend because "love never fails."

Prayer Starter:

❑ Thank Jesus for setting an example as One who managed to lay hands on a few sick people despite an entire town chasing Him away and trying to murder Him.

❑ Ask the Holy Spirit to strengthen your emotional resolve in the midst of friends rejecting you, and ask Him to give you words that might convince them to allow you to persevere.

❑ Pray that the Lord would soften your friends' hearts to allow you to minister healing to them. Pray that they would see Jesus in you and recognize that you carry His Spirit and have healing to offer in Jesus' name.

Journal Experience:

Why do you think it is so common for friends to shy away from our ministry rather than allowing us to persevere in that moment for their healing? What might you be able to say in the moment to respectfully encourage them to let you continue to try?

_____

_____

_____

_____

_____

_____

_____

_____

_____

_____

_____

_____

_____

_____

_____

_____

_____

Action Step:

Find a friend who needs healing and offer to pray for them. Speak to the condition quickly (before they have an opportunity to doubt that you have anything to offer), and immediately ask them to test out their condition. See what happens.

Supplemental Reading:
❏   Luke 4:14-30

DAY 33
MINISTERING TO CO-WORKERS

James Loruss

Before I went into fulltime ministry, I was a working person. I was working for an engineering firm, but I was constantly ministering to people on my job... There were times when I would be ministering – I mean directly saying, "You don't feel good today? Let me pray for you," and there were times where other people in the office would want to come to me and just make jokes. And while they're standing there making jokes – not feeling good, sniffling, or whatever – they would stop. And one time in particular, this guy – he says, "I don't believe it." I said, "What?" He says, "As I'm standing here talking to you, I'm just starting to feel better."

~ Jeff Rogers

Romans 12:14-18 — Bless those who persecute you; bless and do not curse. Rejoice with those who rejoice; mourn with those who mourn. Live in harmony with one another. Do not be proud, but

> be willing to associate with people of low position. Do not be conceited. Do not repay anyone evil for evil. Be careful to do what is right in the eyes of everyone. If it is possible, as far as it depends on you, live at peace with everyone.
>
> **Colossians 3:23** — Whatever you do, work at it with all your heart, as working for the Lord, not for human masters. (NIV)

For the past couple years, I've worked part-time at an automotive plant. It has been a great place for ministry because I get to work with the same people every day whether they like it or not! Recently, we had a seasonal employee in our department, and he was having issues with his shoulders. This guy didn't know me super well, but he knew me well enough to know I'm a Christian and I believe in healing.

One day, he started to complain about the pain he was having and — kind of jokingly — said in my direction, "Hey James! Can you do some of that voodoo magic healing on my shoulders?"

Now I'm not sure if he was making fun of me or genuinely calling out for prayer, but it didn't matter to me. I immediately responded, "Of course! Watch this!" I grabbed his shoulder and said, "Be healed in Jesus' name," and had him test it out.

He freaked out and yelled "No way!" Laughing nervously, he said the shoulder I laid my hands on was all better but the other one still hurt. Without a chance for him to say no, I put my hand on his other shoulder and commanded the pain to leave. He tested that one and it too was totally healed. I told Him that the same power that just healed his shoulders paid for his sin too.

When you're ministering on the job, there are a few factors to consider. First, remember that even though you're a servant of God first, you are in your place of employment because you have made a commitment to help earn money for a company. In other words, be sure to fulfill your work responsibilities with professionalism and excellence. In this way, you'll have favor with your employer and be in a better position if co-workers start complaining about your ministry on the job. Second, whenever possible, try to relegate ministry that takes longer than a normal social interaction to your own time—on breaks, at lunch, or after work. Do what you're being paid to do when you're being paid to do it (so that you're not stealing), but keep your Christian witness alive at all times. And third, remember that you are at all times representing Jesus, whether you're ministering healing or doing your work. Work with all your heart, strive to live at peace with everyone (your co-workers, your subordinates, and your employer), and look for ways to serve others.

It doesn't matter if you're the CEO of a company or a bag boy at the local grocery store—God will use your employment for His glory. I've found that simply walking in obedience and enjoying God's presence actually invite miracles and healing. Walk in love and obedience, and watch what God does wherever you go.

Prayer Starter:

❑ If you have a job, praise God for giving it to you. If you're looking for a job, thank God for the one He has in store for you. And if you're not looking for employment, thank Him that you're able to devote so much time to the other things He has called you to do.

❑ Ask God for a greater desire to listen for His voice and obey Him. Ask Him to make you the best employee in your place of work.

❑ Ask the Holy Spirit to open doors in your sphere of influence to minister to others while still representing the excellence and servitude of Jesus in everything you do.

Journal Experience:

Before entering ministry, Jesus was either a carpenter or a stonemason (depending on your translation of the Greek word). In either profession, Jesus would have been responsible to make business transactions, earn a profit, and produce quality work to sustain His home life. And before He owned His own business, He would have apprenticed under his earthly father, Joseph, as a sort of "subordinate." Take a moment to think about how Jesus would have conducted business—His attitudes, His work ethic, and His priorities. Write down some of your thoughts.

_____

_____

Action Step:

Ask God to bring one person in the workforce to your attention (either in your own place of employment or someone else who is on the job somewhere that you might be, like a store clerk, gas station attendant, or wait-staff at a restaurant). Before He tells you what to do or say, decide that you will say, "Yes," regardless of what He asks. Then look for the opportunity, listen for Him to give you an idea of what to do or say, and respond in obedience. Have fun!

Supplemental Reading:
❏ 2 John 1:6

DAY 34
MINISTERING TO STRANGERS

Jonathan Ammon

Do what you would want done to you. If you knew that someone was walking down the aisle at Walmart, and you had a physical problem, and they had what it took to set you free, you would hope that they would do that for you! So, you know, love them like you would want to be loved, and just pray for them. And – like a normal person – love them and do your best. Start where you're at.

~ Josh Greeson

Acts 3:1-8 — One day Peter and John were going up to the temple at the time of prayer—at three in the afternoon. Now a man who was lame from birth was being carried to the temple gate called Beautiful, where he was put every day to beg from those going into the temple courts. When he saw Peter and John about to enter, he asked them for money. Peter looked straight at him, as did John. Then Peter said, "Look at us!" So the man gave them his attention, expecting to get something from them.

Then Peter said, "Silver or gold I do not have, but what I do have I give you. In the name of Jesus Christ of Nazareth, walk." Taking him by the right hand, he helped him up, and instantly the man's feet and ankles became strong. He jumped to his feet and began to walk. Then he went with them into the temple courts, walking and jumping, and praising God. (NIV)

One night while I was out walking, the Lord directed me to two gentlemen — one was a Muslim man who had a broken leg. I ended up talking to them and sharing my testimony. They were both impacted by the testimony and had lots of questions.

The one with the broken leg said, "It's hard to believe miracles."

Oh, yeah?" I replied, "What about your foot? What happened?"

He said he was in a car accident. I asked if it hurt, and he said, "Yes."

"Ok, well, if I pray for you, and the pain goes away, then you'll know God does miracles, right?"

He agreed. I asked if I could put my hand on his leg, and then I prayed.

"How's it feel?" I asked.

"It still hurts"

"Can I pray, again?"

"Sure."

I put my hand on his leg and prayed again. I looked up, and his eyes were huge.

"It's psychology! It's psychology!" he

exclaimed.

"What's psychology? Is the pain gone in your leg?"

"It's because I saw you do it!" he rationalized, "It's all in my brain!" He refused to believe it even though God had set him up.

I laughed. "Ok, I won't call it a miracle until you check it out; but if you find out your leg isn't broken anymore, you'll know God did a miracle for you."

"Ok, yeah, that's right." He nodded. He looked strangely relieved.

I went on to share the Gospel with both of them, and we had a long conversation.

There are a number of things to consider when ministering to strangers. Each time you approach someone you don't know, remember that God does know them, and He can direct your words and actions if you purpose in your heart to let Him love through you.

When the person you approach does not know Jesus, you have to realize that they don't believe in the Gospel, let alone healing. The healing is a sign to them, and it is probably something they are not seeking. You have to offer it to them, knowing that they will not understand until they are touched by Christ's power.

Other times, the strangers you meet are other believers who may look at you as a "kooky charismatic" who wants to pressure them into some kind of faith-healing fantasy world. In the same way you would approach a lost person with kindness and compassion, these people need to know that you truly care for them and genuinely believe that this will work. They may also need you to be down-to-earth and "normal" enough in your demeanor for them to trust you.

You may even find yourself ministering to believers who do not know you but do believe in healing and therefore have great expectation of you. They may look at you as a powerful healing minister or a man or woman of God who is supplying healing power in a way that they need.

In every case you must lift up the name of Jesus boldly like Peter and John declaring to all that faith in the name of Jesus makes the sick person well (Acts 3:12-16). Compassion and humility are disarming for unbelieving strangers, and these are also a healthy balancing measure for those who view you as a powerful servant of God. Compassion and humility cannot be faked, and through them, people will encounter Jesus. And that's your role whenever you approach a stranger: introduce them to the person of Jesus Christ. They may never meet you again, but they're sure to meet Jesus again.

Prayer Starter:

❑ Worship God, and acknowledge His great love and compassion for those who do not know Him. Thank Him that He paid the price for every human being and that He loves all equally.

❑ Ask Him to give you His heart for strangers and to give you genuine care for those you don't know. Ask Him to increase your compassion.

❑ Contemplate the suffering of others. Think about how you would feel if you were paralyzed and the person in the next aisle of the supermarket had access to the cure for your paralysis. Ask God to empower and embolden you to do for others what you would want them to do for you.

Journal Experience:

What do you consider to be the most intimidating aspect of approaching a stranger to pray for healing? Ask the Lord how to overcome that issue, and write down any solutions that come to mind.

Action Step:

Either keep your eye out for people with obvious physical conditions today, or simply offer to pray for everyone you can, ministering healing to those who need it. When you see obvious conditions (like a cast, crutches, or a wheelchair), the easiest approach is often to ask the person, "What's your story?" or, "What happened?" And once you have listened intently to their story, ask if you can pray for them.

Supplemental Reading:
❑   John 5:1-15

Day 35
Ministering to Yourself

James Loruss

The worst thing we can do is blame God – either to say God sent the disease or to say God didn't allow [healing] to happen. That isn't true... God didn't send cancer to teach me a lesson; He sent Jesus to teach cancer a lesson.

~ *Paul Manwaring*

Mark 5:25-29 — And a woman was there who had been subject to bleeding for twelve years. She had suffered a great deal under the care of many doctors and had spent all she had, yet instead of getting better she grew worse. When she heard about Jesus, she came up behind him in the crowd and touched his cloak, because she thought, "If I just touch his clothes, I will be healed." Immediately her bleeding stopped and she felt in her body that she was freed from her suffering. (NIV)

Think about it: this woman had been suffering for years. She could have thought by now, "This is just the way things are going to be." She had probably lost all hope.

But then, she heard about this "Jesus" who is healing the sick. She knew this was probably her only chance.

"If I just touch his clothes," she thought, "I will be healed."

It was dangerous. A woman with blood issues was considered "unclean" by the Law. To touch anyone was forbidden—let alone a Rabbi. Nonetheless, it was worth the risk. She reached out, touched Jesus, and instantly the bleeding stopped.

This woman had a problem, and she knew that Jesus was the solution. Without help from anyone else, she pressed forward to touch Jesus.

Most of this book has consisted of tips and teaching regarding ministering healing to others, but what happens if *you* get sick?

There are two solutions, and both involve touching Jesus. The first way is to recognize that the fullness of Jesus lives in every Christian you know. They are part of His body, and touching them is just like touching Jesus. Ask other believers to pray for you (James 5:14-15).

The second way to minister healing to yourself is simply the same way that you pray for someone else.

One of my family members was activated in healing ministry this way. My older brother works on a lot of construction sites. One day, he was on a job working with concrete mix, which can cause serious problems if it gets into your skin and especially in your eyes. Some of the dust blew into his left eye, which caused intense pain.

My brother went home and tried to flush it out with water, but nothing was working. He thought he was going to have to take a trip to the emergency room because he couldn't open his eye. Then he remembered some healing teaching, put his hand on his eye, and said, "Eye, be healed."

Instantly, all the pain left, and his eye was perfectly fine!

In 1 Corinthians 6:19-20, Paul tells us that our bodies are temples of the Holy Spirit. You were bought at a price: the blood of Jesus. If there is sickness in your body, you have the authority to tell it to leave. And if you're struggling to see results, be sure to make opportunities for Jesus to touch you through other believers.

Prayer Starter:

❑ Thank Jesus for purchasing your body and taking away any authority the devil could have had over it.

❑ Ask the Lord to build up your faith to expect that He wants to heal you, and that He will even do it through your own words of authority.

❑ Ask God to help you see Jesus in the Christians around you so that you will genuinely expect to encounter Him through their lives.

Journal Experience:

Do you find it easier to minister healing to others or to yourself? Why? Ask the Lord to give you encouragement that will help increase your faith for whichever side is lacking. Write down any encouraging thoughts that come to mind.

_____

_____

_____

_____

_____

_____

_____

_____

_____

_____

_____

_____

_____

_____

_____

_____

_____

Action Step:

As you're reading this, you will fit into one of two categories: Either you need physical healing or you don't. If you don't, praise God for a healthy body! But if you do need to be healed, put your hand wherever the issue is right now. Simply say, "Be healed in Jesus' name." Now test it out! Remember: remain persistent, and choose to rest in the fact that Jesus wants you to be healed.

Supplemental Reading:
❑   Psalm 16:8-10
❑   Psalm 103:1-5

SECTION 8:
Maturing in the Ministry of Healing

DAY 36
KNOW YOUR IDENTITY

James Loruss

I think identity is key because when you look at the life of Jesus and when He was being baptized in the river Jordan, the heavens opened, and a voice came down and said, "This is My beloved Son in whom I am well pleased." And then it goes on to say that the Spirit leads Him into the desert where He's tempted by the devil. And the devil says this: "If you are the Son of God" – His identity is questioned almost immediately. But this is what the enemy leaves out: beloved. He leaves out "beloved." The enemy doesn't want you to know that you are a son or a daughter. Even more still, he doesn't want you to know that you are loved by your Father in heaven.

~ *Cynthia Beckley*

Galatians 2:20 — I have been crucified with Christ and I no longer live, but Christ lives in me. The life I now live in the body, I live by faith in the Son of God, who loved me and gave himself for me. (NIV)

You are loved. If there's only one thing you take away from this study, know this: You are deeply loved.

When Christ died, He died for your sins once and for all. When He died, your old life died too. The awesome thing is that Christ didn't stay dead, and neither did you! He was raised to new life, and you too are now a new creation (2 Corinthians 5:17)! You are alive and free to be who He has called you to be: a son or daughter of the King. To me, this is the most important lesson. If I know who I am, there is no limit to what I can do within my relationship with God.

Do you realize that the same Spirit that raised Christ from the dead dwells within your body (Romans 8:11)? You have "everything" that you need "for life and godliness" because you know Jesus (2 Peter 1:3). In the next verse, Peter continues, "Through these [God's glory and goodness] He has given us His very great and precious promises, so that through them you may participate in the divine nature, having escaped the corruption in the world caused by evil desires." It is your inheritance to participate in the divine nature of our Lord. You do not have to be corrupted by the world around you.

Through Christ, we have been made righteous, and we stand blameless before His presence. The devil has nothing on you. Your identity is in Christ and Christ alone. Your old identity — your identity of sin — was crucified with Him, and you no longer live. Now Christ lives in you (Galatians 2:20). You sit with Him on His throne (Ephesians 2:6). You too — whether male or female — are a son of God. You have been given God's glory and goodness so that you can participate in His divine nature. His nature has become your nature because your sinful nature has been crucified.

When it comes to healing ministry, knowing your identity has two valuable effects. First, it produces confidence for immediate healing and also strengthens your resolve that perseverance will be effective because you know the authority and power you carry in Christ despite any lack of results in the moment. And second, it keeps you from becoming discouraged if things don't seem to be happening. If you try to find your identity in success rates or numbers of healings, then your life will be an emotional rollercoaster. But if you determine to find your identity in Jesus alone, then circumstances won't shake you.

Prayer Starter:

- ❑ Praise God for being a good Father to you.
- ❑ Thank God that He calls you beloved
- ❑ Pray for other believers to realize their true identity in Christ

Journal Experience:

First, write down a handful of things that you know are true about the identity of Jesus.

_____

_____

_____

_____

_____

_____

_____

_____

_____

_____

Now, ask God this simple question: "What do You think of me?" Write down anything He speaks to you.

_____

_____

_____

_____

_____

_____

_____

_____

_____

_____

_____

_____

_____

_____

_____

_____

Finally, think about what you believe God spoke to you about His thoughts toward you. Do these sound like Jesus? Are they Biblical? Write down how these thoughts make you feel and how they will affect you in healing ministry.

_____

_____

_____

_____

_____

_____

_____

_____

_____

_____

Action Step:

Your identity is solely in Christ. If you can't find something in the life of Jesus, get it out of your life. First, take a moment to ask God, "Is there anything you want to reveal in my life that is not of You?" What is He saying? Respond accordingly, and allow Him to encourage you in your true identity.

Supplemental Reading:
❑   Colossians 3:12-14
❑   Romans 6:5-14

DAY 37
GROW IN YOUR RELATIONSHIP WITH JESUS

Jonathan Ammon

Everything emanates from relationship. There's no formula. When I do Healing Schools, we don't teach particular ways to heal people because there is no particular way. It all emanates from relationship. And I would encourage anyone who wants to enter into this: You must be in relationship with Him, and you must understand that it's really about Him and not you.

~ Les Coombs

John 5:19-21 — Jesus gave them this answer: "Very truly I tell you, the Son can do nothing by Himself; He can do only what He sees His Father doing, because whatever the Father does the Son also does. For the Father loves the Son and shows Him all He does. Yes, and He will show Him even greater works than these, so that you will be amazed. For just as the Father raises the dead and gives them

life, even so the Son gives life to whom He
is pleased to give it. (NIV)

Jesus was clear about His complete dependence upon the Father. In the same way that Jesus was dependent upon the Father for healing and miracles, we are dependent on our relationship with Christ. You too can only do what you see the Father doing, and Jesus is the perfect revelation of the Father.

Our proximity to Jesus impacts our perspective. As we behold Him, we are transformed into His image (2 Corinthians 3:18). This process continues until we see Him in all His fullness and then become like Him in all His fullness (1 John 3:2).

When we "strive" and "contend" for greater results in healing ministry, we are not trying to grasp something that God is unwilling to give us. And we are not trying to earn power or gifts by our work or effort. Rather, we are putting effort and strength into our relationships with Jesus. We are denying all distractions in order to be closer to Him — to see Him more clearly and to thereby become more like Him. Grace and love compel us to draw close to Him. When we spend more time with the Lord our Healer, our vision of Him overwhelms the physical problems we see in front of us.

The accounts of the disciples' failure to heal and deliver the epileptic boy mention prayer and (in some manuscripts) fasting — not because they were works required to achieve the boy's healing, but because intimacy is required to overcome the unbelief in our hearts. While I never would have admitted it, I used to think that healing power was something we had to work to unlock. Like a video game, I thought a certain combination of Bible reading, confession, prayer, and fasting would fill up the "power bar" until special miracles would be achieved. Now I know that simply being close to Jesus positions me to know and give His power as He holds my hand in His.

The world is dying of sickness and disease. Now is not the time to be lax or to simply hold on to what we have. Today is the day of healing. We must grow into all that Christ has and is.

Prayer Starter:

- ❏ Thank God for being a loving Father who draws near to His children. Ask Him to reveal Himself more clearly. Ask Him to draw you closer and closer to Him.
- ❏ Ask God if there is anything obscuring your fellowship with Him. Ask Him to teach you how to draw closer to Him. Ask Him what you can do right now to grow closer to Him.
- ❏ Ask God to press the needs of others on your heart as you draw close to Him. Ask Him to help you realize that your relationship with God is not just for you, but for others also.

Journal Experience:

What are some ways you can grow in your relationship with Jesus and in your faith?

_____

_____

_____

_____

_____

_____

_____

_____

_____

_____

_____

_____

_____

_____

_____

_____

_____

_____

_____

_____

Action Step:

Jesus named fasting and prayer in conjunction with unbelief as part of the disciples failure with the epileptic boy, but He didn't stop to fast and pray right then. He lived a lifestyle of fasting and prayer. Do you have a lifestyle of prayer and fasting? Set aside some extra time this week to pray. Consider planning a fast. Remember that these things do not earn results in healing ministry, but they are tools for helping you to develop intimacy with the Lord.

Supplemental Reading:
❑   2 Peter 3:17-18
❑   Ephesians 4:14-16
❑   John 13:13-17

DAY 38
DEMONSTRATE THE NATURE OF JESUS

James Loruss (with Art Thomas)

Jesus is normal Christianity, and those that came up to Him were healed.

~ *Robert Ward*

2 Peter 1:3-9 — His divine power has given us everything we need for a godly life through our knowledge of him who called us by his own glory and goodness. Through these he has given us his very great and precious promises, so that through them you may participate in the divine nature, having escaped the corruption in the world caused by evil desires.

For this very reason, make every effort to add to your faith goodness; and to goodness, knowledge; and to knowledge, self-control; and to self-control, perseverance; and to perseverance, godliness; and to

> godliness, mutual affection; and to mutual affection, love. For if you possess these qualities in increasing measure, they will keep you from being ineffective and unproductive in your knowledge of our Lord Jesus Christ. But whoever does not have them is nearsighted and blind, forgetting that they have been cleansed from their past sins. (NIV)

It's not uncommon to see two categories of Christians: (1) Those who love to be like Jesus in His character and nature but are not much like Him in His ministry of power and (2) those who love to be like Jesus in His ministry of power but are not much like Him in His character and nature. Ironically, both sides tend to look at the other extreme and call the other side "un-Christ-like." The fact is, they're both right! If I want to be like Jesus, then I need to be completely like Him in both His nature and His ministry of power. First John 2:6 says, "Whoever claims to live in Him must live as Jesus did."

I'm amazed at the amount of Christians who become upset with me when I contend to be exactly like Jesus. I've heard the arguments: "Well, that was Jesus...You can't expect to see the same results," or, "You're only human. Jesus was God!" None of the excuses I've heard are valid excuses for sinning or contending for less than what Jesus paid for.

I'm human, yes. But what about Jesus? Was He not human as well? "Fully God and fully man" we say. In fact, Scripture shows that He limited Himself when He took on flesh, requiring the power of the Holy Spirit for ministry and being unable to do anything apart from the Father (John 5:19, Acts 10:38, and Philippians 2:6-8). Jesus showed us what a human being can do when he or she is in right relationship with the Father and living sin-free; and then He said we would actually be able to do greater (John 14:12)!

Then, with His own blood, Jesus made this lifestyle possible! He cleansed us from all sin. By dying with Christ, we were set free from sin (Romans 6:6-7). It is just as unnatural for me to sin as it is unnatural (and even unthinkable) for Jesus to sin (1 John 3:9 and 5:18). Furthermore, He gave us His Spirit so that we could be empowered to witness Him wherever we go (Acts 1:8).

The devil would love for me to stay stagnant in my walk with Christ. Satan knows his best tactic against Christians is to keep us happy and comfortable where we are. If he can keep us spiritually lulled to sleep, then he doesn't have to worry about what we'll be doing for the Kingdom of God.

But the truth is that he is terrified of you! When you realize who you are and begin to demonstrate the very nature of Jesus, Satan has no defense. Do not be blinded by his lies. Instead, keep your eyes on Jesus. There you'll find your identity, your satisfaction, and your purpose in life.

As you allow the nature of Jesus to overtake your life, and as you allow Him to reveal Himself through you, people will encounter more than His power—they will encounter Him in His fullness. This world is dying, and people are going to hell. The world needs an encounter with the fullness of Jesus—both His power and His nature—and we are the only ones equipped to bring this encounter. You are called. You are equipped. You are a son or daughter of the living God—ambassadors and representatives of the One who sent you. Go out and bring His kingdom to this earth.

Prayer Starter:

- ❑ Thank Jesus for setting the bar of what is "normal" in the Christian life.
- ❑ Thank God that He sees you with unlimited potential.
- ❑ Ask God to bring a non-believer across your path today with whom you can share the Gospel.

Journal Experience:

Which aspect of your life do you feel looks more like Jesus: Your expression of His nature and character? or your expression of His ministry of power?

Ask the Lord what needs to change in your life so that you can look more like Jesus in both ways. Write down any thoughts that come to mind.

_____

_____

_____

_____

_____

_____

_____

Action Step:

Look for an opportunity to represent Jesus' nature today. Deliberately self-sacrifice for someone, encourage someone, or take time for a person who would otherwise be overlooked or rejected. Ask if they need prayer for anything.

Supplemental Reading:
❏   Mark 16:17-18
❏   John 14:12

DAY 39
TEACH OTHERS TO DO THE SAME

Jonathan Ammon

I think people overcomplicate the issue of healing. I've read books about healing that--when I got finished reading them — I felt less confident and less like I knew what I should do. I've heard people preach about healing; and when they get finished preaching, you'd think that only "super-evangelists" with large ministries are able to see people healed. I think the key is just to simplify: Healing is something that was purchased on the cross. Jesus paid for it. It has nothing to do with our righteousness... It's faith. And everything that you introduce that brings confusion and that brings unbelief only hinders the power of God to heal.

~ Daniel Kolenda

Matthew 28:18-20 — Then Jesus came to them and said, "All authority in heaven and on earth has been given to me. Therefore go and make disciples of all nations, baptizing them in the name of the Father and of the Son and of the Holy Spirit, and teaching them to obey everything I have commanded you. And surely I am with you always, to the very end of the age." (NIV)

2 Timothy 2:2 — And the things that you have heard from me among many witnesses, commit these to faithful men who will be able to teach others also. (NKJV)

Paul instructed Timothy to entrust the valuable Word of God that he had received to others who would continue to spread the kingdom throughout the earth. He instructed Timothy to "commit" the content and the practice of what he had taught him to others who "will be able to teach others also." He had a vision for generations of young men who would carry the ministry throughout the world.

Paul was not simply asking Timothy to pass on mere words or teaching. He was clear that the Kingdom is not a matter of words but of power (1 Corinthians 4:20). The preaching of the Gospel — confirmed by signs of God's compassion, love, and power — was something Paul embodied constantly to the world "among many witnesses."

When Jesus commissioned the Twelve, He instructed them to "make disciples of all nations." And when they made these disciples, they were then to "[teach] them to obey everything I have commanded you." One of the things Jesus had commanded His Twelve to do was to "Heal the sick" (Matthew 10:8). Healing ministry is a command that Jesus intended to be passed from one generation of believers to the next.

The message, practice, and empowerment of every believer to heal the sick must spread from believer to believer. You can commit what has been given to you to those who will be faithful to also lay their hands on the sick and see them recover. By simply teaching one faithful individual to heal the sick, you have doubled the fruit and effectiveness of your ministry—you have doubled the seed of divine healing that Christ has sown into your life, and you have multiplied the potential of seeing God's will done on earth as it is in Heaven.

Jesus said that the Kingdom—the reign and dominion of the Lord our Healer—is like a mustard seed that, though the smallest of seeds, multiplies its cells exponentially to become the largest herb that even the birds in the field nest in (Matthew 13:31-32). He told the parable of the talents, saying that the Kingdom can be compared to a King who invests precious resources to his servants, expecting them to invest and multiply what they have been given (Matthew 25:14-30). Today, you have the opportunity to multiply what you have been given—to pass on the expression of Jesus's healing power that saves lives.

Find faithful men. Commit to them what you have learned. Teach others to heal the sick.

Prayer Starter:

❑ Take a moment to thank the Father for trusting you with such a precious message and such precious power. Thank Him for the contagious spread of the Kingdom.

❑ Ask the Lord to empower and enable you to wisely invest the message of divine healing in others. Ask Him to teach you how to impart your faith in Christ the Healer to others and how to teach others to practically heal the sick.

❑ Ask the Lord to give you faithful people and laborers for the harvest (Luke 10:2). Ask Him to give you those who will receive and pass on the message and practice of divine healing. Ask Him for specific names and specific people to whom you can pass on what you have learned.

Journal Experience:

Is there anything left that you need to know in order to teach others to heal the sick?

_____

_____

_____

What is required of you in order for you to effectively teach others to heal the sick?

_____

_____

_____

_____

_____

_____

What are some opportunities you have or can make for teaching others to heal the sick?

_____

_____

_____

_____

_____

_____

_____

_____

_____

How can you get started today?

_____

_____

_____

_____

_____

Action Step:

Jesus sent out teams of two to preach and heal the sick (Luke 10:1,9). Invite someone to come with you as you go to minister healing to someone. Most of you reading this can call someone right now and make a plan to pray for someone you know who is suffering or to go on the street and pray for strangers. The next time you lay hands on the sick, explain to the people around you what you are doing. Model healing the sick, and point everyone to Jesus.

Supplemental Reading:
❑   Matthew 25:14-30
❑   Matthew 13:23
❑   Matthew 9:35-10:8

DAY 40
LOVE EXTRAVAGANTLY

Jonathan Ammon

That's the biggest thing: "For God so loved the world that He gave His only Son." See, it cost God something – it cost Him His Son. And it cost Jesus something – it cost Him His life. What's it going to cost us? It's going to cost us to go pick up our cross and go love someone, even when it's hard.

~ Kristina Waggoner

John 15:9-17 — As the Father has loved me, so have I loved you. Now remain in my love. If you keep my commands, you will remain in my love, just as I have kept my Father's commands and remain in his love. I have told you this so that my joy may be in you and that your joy may be complete. My command is this: Love each other as I have loved you. Greater love has no one than this: to lay down one's life for one's friends. You are my friends if you do what I command. I no

> longer call you servants, because a servant does not know his master's business. Instead, I have called you friends, for everything that I learned from my Father I have made known to you. You did not choose me, but I chose you and appointed you so that you might go and bear fruit—fruit that will last—and so that whatever you ask in my name the Father will give you. This is my command: Love each other. (NIV)

I was telling a co-missionary about a group of Muslims who were healed the previous week, and he interrupted me to say, "You know what I really appreciate about you? You pray for the sick because you really believe God loves them and wants to heal them, not to just get your foot in the door."

God is love. He has many attributes, but He *is* love. As the God of all creation who holds all things together by the Word of His power, He defined love as the greatest of all things. He defined love as self-sacrifice. He told us to love the world as He loved them, to take up our cross and lay down our lives— not only for the King who loved us first, not only for our brothers and sisters in Christ who share in that love, but for a lost, dying, and hostile world that has never seen or known love. They can know Him through us.

We love God because He first loved us. My heart's desire is that the whole world would love Jesus Christ as I do. I'm in tears writing this, thinking about the lostness of humanity and remembering what it is like to not know hope or love. The whole world is waiting to experience the love of the Father. The whole world is longing for a loving God who will intervene in their lives. God is speaking, yet many never hear His voice. God is reaching out, but many never receive His touch. You are His voice and His touch to this lost and unloved world.

I have seen grown men break down and weep heavily because of God healing a minor shoulder injury—not because their pain is gone, but because a real and living God broke through the natural order in order to intervene in their lives and do something that only He could do. Suddenly, their eyes are opened to a God who loves them and is willing and able to touch and heal. We must become this love. This is what we were born for.

Prayer Starter:

❑ Thank God for His great, great love. Think about how much He loves you. Ask Him to reveal that love in a fresh way right now. Respond to that love.

❑ Turn back in the pages of this book to Day 11. Read out loud the journal entry from that day. Allow the Lord to remind you that you are a personification of love, representing the Ultimate Personification of Love: God Himself.

❑ Ask God to give you a heart that overflows with love for a lost world. Ask Him to reveal His love for the lost.

Journal Experience:

How can you love people with healing ministry? What do you think self-sacrificial healing ministry looks like?

Action Step:

We are commanded to pursue love and earnestly desire spiritual gifts, including healing (1 Corinthians 12:31). Set aside time to pursue God's heart and His love in prayer; then, out of that time, look for opportunities to let His love overflow onto others. Put your answer to the Journal Experience above into practice. Attach the message of God's love to your ministry to the sick. Tell someone, "God loves you," today.

Supplemental Reading:
❑   1 John 4:7-19

What Now?

Congratulations on completing this entire 40-Day journey! We have no doubt that you have been impacted on some level by the teachings and challenges from each day of the study. In fact, we recognize that it's entirely possible that you have had your entire perspective about healing ministry turned upside-down.

There are three things we would like to recommend for you to do next:

1. Watch the movie *Paid in Full* a second time. Many people are so shocked during their first viewing that they miss much of the message. Watching it again — after having completed this study — is sure to be a different experience and may bring out new insights that you had not previously noticed.

2. Consider hosting an 8-week small group study about healing ministry with help from the DVD curriculum available at PaidInFullFilm.com. You can even use this book as supplemental reading that corresponds to each week's lesson.
3. Keep spreading the message of Jesus Christ's power to save, heal, and set free!

It has been an honor to have been welcomed to speak into your life for the past few weeks, and we pray that God guards the seeds that have been planted through this study so that you bear much fruit in His Kingdom. Be blessed as you minister the full Gospel of Jesus Christ wherever He sends you!

Art Thomas
James Loruss
Jonathan Ammon

About the Authors

Art Thomas

Art Thomas is a missionary-evangelist who has preached the Gospel in many diverse settings spanning from the inner city of Brooklyn, New York, to the bush of Africa. Now serving as the president and CEO of *Wildfire Ministries International*, Art has seen hundreds of people come to salvation and thousands physically healed since stepping into itinerant ministry in April of 2011. He is the director and producer of the movie *Paid in Full* and has been actively involved in training hundreds of other people to minister physical healing since 2009.

Art is the author of *The Word of Knowledge in Action: A Practical Guide for the Supernatural Church* and *Spiritual Tweezers: Removing Paul's "Thorn in the Flesh" and Other False Objections to God's Will for Healing.* He lives with his wife, Robin, and their two boys, Josiah and Jeremiah, in Plymouth, Michigan.

James Loruss

James Loruss is the vice president of *Wildfire Ministries International* and is the co-Director of the movie *Paid in Full*. James studied film music scoring at Madonna University, which provided the initial inspiration for the film that he and Art would go on to make—ultimately leading to this book.

James has preached to hundreds in America and thousands in Africa and has been actively involved in healing ministry since 2009. His greatest passions—besides the salvation of the lost—include the Church understanding identity in Christ and the love of the Father. James lives in Novi, Michigan.

Jonathan Ammon

Jonathan Ammon is a ministry associate with *Wildfire Ministries International* who has traveled extensively (in America and Uganda) with Art Thomas and James Loruss and also helped with the filming of the movie, *Paid in Full*. He has devoted the past four years of his life to a 2-square-mile city within downtown Detroit, Michigan, called Hamtramck. Within those 2 square miles are 14 mosques with roughly 40% of the population having been born overseas. It is currently known as the only city in the United States where the Muslim "call to prayer" is openly broadcast five times a day.

Jonathan teaches English as a Second Language to immigrants (mostly from Yemen and Bangladesh) using the Bible as a study tool. He conducts street evangelism, starts Bible studies in homes, and is actively involved in prophetic and healing ministries while training other believers to do the same things in Jesus' name. Most of his efforts are devoted to establishing a movement of evangelistic, self-replicating gatherings of Christians throughout the region that will spread the Gospel faster than the current birth rate.

For more information about
Wildfire Ministries International,
please visit
www.WildfireMin.org

For more information about
Art Thomas Ministries,
please visit
www.ArtThomas.org

APPENDIX A:
12 Traits of a Healthy Healing Ministry

Art Thomas

While I've only been personally engaged in healing ministry for a few years, I spent my entire life among Pentecostal and Charismatic Christians. Healing ministry was something we believed in. But over the course of nearly thirty years in this movement, I've witnessed various healing ministers slipping into pitfalls that have either derailed their ministries or brought them under public reproach.

These observations have led me to incorporate a handful of "guideposts" in my life and ministry to help me ensure that I'm on-track with representing Jesus in everything I do.

The following list offers twelve traits of a healthy healing ministry. Naturally, there are more that could be added to this list, but I have chosen these twelve because of their usefulness to effective healing ministry and how commonly they have been neglected by various healing ministers throughout history.

Each of the following traits should be read and processed through the lens of grace — recognizing that Jesus has already placed these things in our lives by virtue of the fact that they are in Him and He is in us. Each topic is a description of what you already look like on the inside because Jesus lives there. The process of working out our salvation involves allowing what we already look like on the inside to be seen on the outside, and this requires the life-long decision to consider yourself dead to sin but alive in Christ (Romans 6:11-14). When God shows you through His word what you look like, you are responsible to live accordingly. To live any differently is to forget what God says you look like (James 1:22-25).

Consider these twelve traits as they relate to your own practice of healing ministry, and ask the Holy Spirit to help you develop them so that the fullness of Jesus can be seen through your life.

1) Faith

Faith is a relational word (see Appendix C). It implies that you wholeheartedly trust God to be who He says He is and to do what He wants to do. Faith is at the core of everything we do in healing ministry and is — generally speaking — the determining factor between either seeing results or people remaining the same. If you do not trust God, you will rarely see

Him heal apart from His own sovereign choice. Conversely, if you have perfect faith like Jesus, then you will see Him heal every single time. Thankfully, Jesus is the One who is authoring and perfecting our faith (Hebrews 12:2). In Second Thessalonians 1:3, Paul thanks God for the believers "because your faith is growing more and more." Faith grows. Allow Jesus to stretch and grow the measure of faith that He has already given you for healing ministry, and you will find yourself trusting God in situations that used to seem impossible.

2) Hope

Hope is the certain expectation of good in the future. Our hope is certain because our God is faithful. Our hope is in Him, and the result is that our thoughts and emotions are anchored to Him (Hebrews 6:19). The more fixated we become on the hope that we have in Christ, the more fully we can endure earthly trials. Jesus Himself endured the torture of Roman crucifixion because He was looking forward to the joy of rescuing us from darkness, setting us free from sin, and transforming us into sons of God (Hebrews 12:2). Be certain of the hope you have — that God loves you and will welcome you into heaven — so that no earthly circumstance or persecution or lack of healing will discourage you from your mission.

3) Love

Faith may be the determining factor between results

and stagnancy, and hope may be the anchor that keeps us tethered to the reality of eternity, but love is the single most important aspect of healing ministry because only through love can we reveal the heart of God (1 Corinthians 13:13). God is love personified (1 John 4:8 and 4:16). No matter how many miracles our faith may produce, without love, we are nothing because the substance of God's Personhood is not being conveyed (1 Corinthians 13:2). Choose to self-sacrifice for others. Serve them, support them, and honor them above yourself. In this way, people will encounter more than the power of Jesus — they will experience the very Person of God through you.

4) Gratitude

One of the greatest struggles in healing ministry is remaining in a posture of gratitude. It's easy to thank and praise God when you're seeing results, but it's very difficult when nothing appears to be happening. When you're not seeing people healed, thank Jesus for the price He paid at the cross as though you had just seen a person leap out of a wheelchair. Furthermore, as you're ministering healing, thank God for every sliver of improvement you see. Thank Him out loud so that the person receiving ministry can be drawn into your worship and be made aware that God is doing something.

5) Perseverance

Perseverance is needed in both short-term situations

and long-term. The short-term scenarios include the times when you speak once to a condition and see nothing happen, so you pray again. The long-term scenarios, though, go beyond persevering in ministry without seeing results. Long-term trials include ridicule, discouragement, people planting seeds of doubt in your heart, persecution, unanswered questions, and more. Never allow these things to have more influence on your life, ministry, and theology than Jesus Christ. Keep your focus on Him, the price He paid, and the hope you have, and you'll find the Lord meeting you with grace to persevere.

6) Gentleness

Gentleness is an expression of the Holy Spirit (Galatians 5:22). When Jesus was confronting hypocritical religious leaders, unbelief in people, or moneychangers in the Temple, He was anything but gentle. Such works of the enemy deserved His fiery correction. But when it came to His ministry to the lost and the hurting, Jesus wasn't a terrifying, imposing force. Children ran to Him—a situation that doesn't happen to grumpy or harsh people. In Jesus' healing ministry, perhaps the least gentle thing He did was rubbing spit-mud in the eyes of a blind man; but this seems to be an exception to the rule. Jesus was gentle and humble in heart (Matthew 11:29). If you wish to represent Him in healing ministry, determine not to make role models out of ministers from the past who kicked and punched people to bring God's healing power (even though it worked for them). Rather, determine to make Jesus your one and only Role Model. Become a person to whom children want to run.

7) Joy

I was preaching in an African village where the head witch-doctor for the region lived. A crowd of people from the village had flocked to hear me speak, and after presenting the Gospel, I jumped off our makeshift stage and began laying hands on the people who had pressed forward for prayer. I noticed one local pastor struggling to cast a demon out of a woman. As I approached them, I began to think about how puny this stubborn demon was compared to the awesome God I serve, and this caused me to laugh. When the demon saw me laugh, the woman began backing up in fear. That made me even happier, and I laughed even more! I said, "You can't stop joy! Now come out of her!" The woman was instantly set free. God sits in heaven and laughs at His enemies (Psalm 2:4). Joy is a great indicator for whether we truly believe God is more powerful than the circumstances we face. As a side note, the head-witchdoctor's wife came to salvation after witnessing the powerful deliverances in that village!

8) Humility

The Bible says that Moses was more humble than anyone else on the face of the earth (Numbers 12:3). Do you know who wrote that book of the Bible? Moses! Humility has nothing to do with putting yourself down or pretending to be nothing. Humility is believing what God says about you despite what you may think or feel. If God says you're the most humble person, and you say you're not, then that's pride because you're exalting your own opinion above God's. So whatever God says about you is true, and you need to embrace it. The Bible doesn't say that you shouldn't think highly of yourself. It simply says, "Do not think of yourself more highly than you ought, but rather think of yourself with sober judgment, in accordance with the faith God has distributed to each of you" (Romans 12:3).

9) Faithfulness

Far too many healing ministries have been derailed by unfaithfulness. The most common form seems to be marital or sexual unfaithfulness, but there are also those who have been unfaithful with ministry money, unfaithful with personal responsibilities, unfaithful with their time, and unfaithful in their relationship with the Lord. Few things will put an end to a minister's credibility in the eyes of the world like unfaithfulness. Faithfulness can seem like a thankless trait because the jaded public generally won't praise you for it until after you die. But it is still one of the character traits of Jesus, and it belongs as a top priority for every minister of healing.

10) Honesty & Integrity

I find it unfortunate that evangelists and "faith-healers" have been branded as people who inflate good news and deflate bad news. It seems as though even our fellow Christian expect us to report more salvations and healings than actually happened or to report fewer losses than actually occurred. But it is vital that we live above reproach. One of the first things that impressed me about Pastor Paul Basuule when I visited his home and ministry in Uganda was that I found everything exactly as he had reported it to me, right down to the number: the size of his congregation, the number of churches he had planted, the number of pastors he was training, and more. Pastor Paul's honesty and integrity endeared me to him and God has shown his ministry tremendous favor as a result. Make sure that every number you report and every testimony you share is completely true to the best of your knowledge. Be honest about things you're not sure about, and set an example of integrity for other believers to look up to.

11) Holiness

Our perspectives on holiness tend to err toward one of two extremes. At one end of the spectrum, we have the hyper-legalists who have lost the motivation of love and believe they are justified before God by their deliberate actions of separation from the world (many times resulting in such unnecessary isolation that they become ineffective at touching the lives of people in the world). At the other end of the spectrum are those who are so enamored with the grace of God and His consistent mercy that they see holy living as being overrated. While there is much more to say about holiness than can be fit into one paragraph, the simple truth is that it is valuable for the healing minister — firstly because it sharpens our spiritual discernment (as darkness feels more abrasive to our spirits), and secondly because it reveals the purity of Jesus to those around us. God commands us, "Be holy, because I am holy" (1 Peter 1:16). This isn't because we can't approach Him without being cleaned up first. Rather it is because we are called to represent Him in this world. He is holy, and we look most like Him when we too are holy.

12) Tact

When I first discovered healing ministry, I was so thrilled by the fact that I finally knew the truth that I was vocally abrasive about it. I would say things with the deliberate intention of offending those who believed differently. It wasn't that I was intending to be a jerk — I just wanted to shake my fellow Christians into believing in the same powerful Jesus I had encountered. In some ways, it worked, and many people around me had their eyes opened (much like blasting a person with a floodlight when their eyes have adjusted to the dark). But in the process, I also burned some bridges and lost some good friends. Declaring God's will to always heal and the reality of our own faith as the main factor for success can be an emotionally difficult pill to swallow — especially for those who have lost loved ones to sickness or disease. In hindsight, I wish I had shown more tact, and I have since allowed the Lord to correct that shortcoming in me. Hopefully, this book has been an example to you for how to preach the truth without compromise in ways that are palatable and gentle to the person with wounds in their hearts.

Develop these traits in your life, and you're sure to see your healing ministry flourish in ways that transcend mere miracles.

APPENDIX B:

Core Practices for Ministering Healing

Art Thomas

There is no set method for conducting healing ministry, but there are some general principles that are helpful tools when you're unsure what to do next.

Wherever the word "minister" is used in this section, it refers to laying hands on the person and/or speaking a word of authority. These principles are a "default" of sorts, based on the example of Jesus and His disciples in the Bible. If the Holy Spirit instructs you to do something else, then obedience to His voice becomes the form of ministry.

The following list of "core practices" are titled as such because they are the foundation on which successful healing ministry can function. None of these principles is a requirement for seeing healing, but we have found them to be helpful in the actual practice of healing ministry. Our hope in presenting them here is to offer very practical advice that will help you experience success in healing ministry and avoid some of the problems from which we have learned.

Relational Approach

Keep things friendly, non-threatening, and upbeat. Smile. Look the person in the eye. Ask permission to lay hands on the person. Feel free to explain what you're doing or chat with the person while you lay hands on them. All of the cultural things we often like to do as Pentecostals or Charismatics during healing ministry (like shouting, jumping, speaking in tongues, shaking, pushing, etc.) are completely unnecessary when it comes to what brings results. You can be very quiet, happy, and "ordinary" and still see God do the miraculous through you.

Test the Condition

Before you begin, ask if there are any symptoms that, if they went away, the person would know they're healed.

In many cases, there is an immediate symptom that can be tested: pain, blindness, deafness, immobility, etc. In these instances, begin with a baseline assessment. If it's pain, for instance, ask them to rate the pain on a scale of one to ten (something many people are used to doing for doctors). If it's blurry eyesight, ask them to look around for something they can test their vision on. How far can they see now? Establish what the person cannot currently do, and then begin ministry.

After ministering to the person, ask them to test their condition. How does it compare? Has there been any change?

One of my favorite questions is, "Is it 100% complete?" Many people will be so happy to have relief that they are satisfied with a partial healing. I tell people that Jesus paid for 100%, and He deserves 100%; then I continue to minister and test things again until the person says their symptoms are completely gone.

In some cases, a condition cannot be tested immediately (like digestive tract issues, allergies, asthma, internal cancer, or diabetes). In these instances, simply minister once, and then ask the person how they feel. Ask them to check their condition later (seeing a doctor if appropriate) and to let you know what happens.

Keep Things Short

Long prayers are almost always unnecessary. In fact, I've learned that in most cases, the faster I minister, the better. Jesus warned us not to pray like the pagans who think they'll be heard because of their many words (Matthew 6:7-8).

In fact, be open to the possibility of God healing a person before you even have the opportunity to minister to them. Listen for the Holy Spirit to prompt you about these scenarios and learn to call them out by asking the person if they're already healed.

Simply place a hand on the person, command the healing briefly, and have the person test it out right away. You'll be amazed how many healings happen that quickly. This also helps keep ministry from taking forever if we find that we need to minister more than once to the person.

Recognizing What God is Doing

Occasionally when I'm ministering healing to someone and I ask them what's happening, they will tell me that they feel heat or electricity around their affected body part (or sometimes throughout their entire body). When this happens, I tell them, "Good. It sounds like God is doing something. So we're just going to let Him do what He's doing, and you can let me know when the sensation stops.

If I'm ministering in a meeting where multiple people are waiting for prayer, I'll use this as an opportunity to pray for someone else. I'll instruct the person to wait there and let God keep working while I pray for someone else, and I assure them that I'll check back in a moment. Every so often, while ministering to the second person, I'll ask the first, "What's happening?" to keep a running assessment of their condition.

When I'm not in a meeting and am alone with the person or on the streets somewhere, I'll usually keep my hand on the area being affected and use the time to chat with the person and explain what's happening.

Typically, once God takes over in this way,

there's nothing left for me to do. He'll complete the healing without my help. But such experiences with the fiery or electric power of God can sometimes be scary for the person, so my presence becomes a reassuring reminder that things are still under control and everything is okay.

Model Gratitude

Every time you see the least bit of change, verbally thank the Lord for what He's doing. This will teach the person to express their own gratitude to God whenever they experience the slightest improvement. I have seen many times when a healing was completed while we were still thanking Him. In fact, I know many people who use gratitude as their preferred method of ministering healing (you may remember Josh MacDonald in our movie grabbing a man's ankle and saying, "Thank You, Father, for a brand new ankle in Jesus' name").

What to do When Pain Moves or Intensifies

Of the thousands of healings I've witnessed, I've seen more than a hundred situations where the pain in the person's body moved from one place to another. Whenever this happens, we know that it's not a normal medical condition. Rather, a demon is behind it, and it just tried to escape what God was doing in one area by scurrying to another.

On a few occasions, I've seen the pain intensify. One woman came to me with fibromyalgia, and when I started to minister to her, the pain became so unbearable that she couldn't stand. I grabbed a chair for her and continued to minister. She cried, "It's too much! I want to stop!" I replied, "I can leave you in this condition if that's what you want, but wouldn't you rather be free?" After about four or five minutes telling the spirit to leave, it came out, and the woman was completely relieved.

Any time the pain moves or intensifies in response to healing ministry, it's a dead giveaway that a demon is at work. When that happens, immediately command the spirit to leave, and ask the person what's happening.

If it moves again or intensifies again, then command it to leave again. Repeat this until it's complete (see Appendix F for more information).

If the symptoms stop, alleviate, or remain the same, I assume that the demon is gone and return to ministering healing. Many times after telling a demon to leave, the person's pain remained the same, but I was then able to tell the affected part to be healed and see results.

Using Words of Knowledge

There are many expressions and uses of the spiritual gift known as a "Word of Knowledge." If you're particularly interested in studying this topic, please refer to the book I wrote titled *The Word of Knowledge in Action: A Practical Guide for the Supernatural Church*, published by Destiny Image Publishers, 2011.

For the purposes of this study on healing ministry, this brief crash course will be sufficient.

A Word of Knowledge happens when the

Holy Spirit takes something Jesus knows and makes it known to you. One of the ways He does this in healing ministry is to cause you to become aware of a particular body part by causing you to feel warmth, tingling, or occasionally even pain in the same area where the person is affected. Another way is simply through information dropped in your mind that you somehow know without any earthly explanation as to why you know it.

Words of Knowledge are extremely useful in healing ministry. One of their greatest values is that they build faith in both the person receiving ministry and in you as the minister. Furthermore, acting on a Word of Knowledge is an expression of obedience, which positions you in submission to God, allowing His authority to flow freely through you.

Obedience producing authority is the whole point. We know that God wants to heal every person in the room, but He sometimes gives a Word of Knowledge so that we have a practical opportunity to submit ourselves to Him in obedience. Whenever I call out a condition through a Word of Knowledge, I know that healing will happen—not because God just told me the only condition He wants to heal but because I know I'm honoring the flow of authority by yielding in obedience to Him. This positions me to speak with His authority and see the healing take place.

Knowing When and How to Back Off

There are seven basic reasons to stop a healing ministry session:

1) The person is healed.
2) The person asks you to stop.
3) You can tell that the person is wanting to stop but is perhaps trying to be polite, so you offer them a way out and they take it.
4) The schedule or venue requires for you to stop or move on.
5) The Holy Spirit is specifically telling you to do something else.
6) You're exhausted physically and emotionally and recognize your own need to rest.
7) You notice that you've stepped outside of faith and started striving in your own effort or pride (trying to achieve results for the sake of looking good, feeling good, or some other selfish reason), and you recognize that you're unable to snap out of it.

The first five scenarios are fairly straightforward to navigate. The last two leave you with some options.

My first act is usually to bring in reinforcements. I'll either ask the Holy Spirit to bring someone to my attention, or I'll simply ask the first person I see if they want to try. Often times, I'll see if there's a little child standing by, and I'll ask if they would like to try. Kids usually jump at the opportunity even when they've been watching things not work for you.

Whoever you have take over for you, coach them through the process and show them what to do. In most cases, I've seen healing work after this.

As a final resort, I'll look the person in the eye and say, "Alright. I'm recognizing that I'm not ministering in faith right now for some reason. If Jesus had touched you, you'd be healed by now; instead, I touched you. But I am absolutely convinced that God wants you to be healed. So I want to encourage you to have Christians continue to minister to you until you're 100% free. You can even speak to the condition yourself. If you want me to keep trying, I'd be happy to, but I need to be honest when I'm recognizing my own moments of weakness."

Ministering to Children

Imagine being a helpless child who's not feeling well physically. Mom or dad scoops you up, and — usually with concern on their face — carries you to a total stranger who lays hands on you and starts shouting in a language you don't know. That's a terrifying experience!

As the minister, there are several things you can do to eliminate the intimidation factor and put the child at ease.

First, smile. Greet the child with an excited expression and say, "Hi there!"

If the child is walking when they're brought to you, immediately stoop down to a kneeling position so that they can meet you on their level.

If the child is vocal enough, try to engage in a little small talk. Tell them your name and ask for theirs. Notice any toys they might be carrying or perhaps a character on their clothing. Then ask with a smile, "What can I pray for you about?"

Many times, the parents will explain the situation. If you're on the ground with the child, stay there and look up at the parents. Whether the parents or the child explain the condition, look back to the child and ask them, "How do you feel right now?" This will help you establish your baseline for testing later. If it's not a testable condition, it will at least express that you care for the child.

Ask the child if it's okay for you to put your hand on them. Be specific about where you intend to place your hand. Then ask the parents, "Is that alright?"

If it's not okay with either the child or the parents, don't worry about it, and move on.

Still smiling, happy, and looking the child in the eye, speak words of authority to the condition in soft, gentle tones. Sicknesses and demons are not intimidated by the volume or intensity of your voice; they're intimidated by the fact that you sit on the throne with Jesus (Ephesians 2:6). There is no need to minister fear to a child while you're trying to minister healing!

If the condition can be tested, ask the child if they want to test it out. Some are very shy and want to stay clinging to mom or dad, and that's okay. In these cases, I tell the parents, "That's fine. Have her check it out later, and if the problem is still there, do the same thing I just did and check it out again."

When finished, thank the child for letting you pray for him or her. Tell them that they did a great job. And whenever the child will go for it, try to end with a high-five, fist-bump, or hand shake.

APPENDIX C:

The Difference Between Faith and Belief

Art Thomas

Faith and belief are two different things, but both are valuable in healing ministry. Jesus said that the sign of healing ministry "will accompany those who *believe*" (Mark 16:17-18). Beyond that, though, we learn that the only time healing ministry didn't work in Scripture was because the disciples lacked *faith* (Matthew 17:20).

It is clear that both faith and belief play a role in healing ministry, but they are still two different things.

Defining Faith

I have faith in my wife, Robin. If she says that she will do something or be somewhere, I know without a doubt that it's true. She's trustworthy, and that gives me the liberty to trust her implicitly. That's called faith.

Suppose my wife calls my phone and tells me that she's meeting friends at a certain restaurant, and I should join them. I know for certain that if I go to that restaurant, she'll be there. But suppose I believe she'll be at another restaurant despite what she said. If that's the case, I'll go to the other restaurant; and I could believe with all my heart that she'll come, but she simply won't. In this case, I allowed an incorrect belief to trump my faith in my wife.

The Bible says that "faith comes from what is heard, and what is heard comes through the word of Christ" (NRSV). In my restaurant analogy, faith was connected to hearing the voice of my wife. In Christianity, faith comes from hearing the voice of Jesus. The more certain I am that Jesus has told me a thing, the more likely I am to completely entrust myself to Him in obedience.

The surest way to know what Jesus has said is to read the Bible. Peter called Scripture "a more sure word of prophecy" (2 Peter 1:19, KJV). In the Bible, we encounter the proven words of God. And as we read about Jesus in the Gospels, we encounter the most complete revelation of the Father to mankind. Read your Bible, and in time, you'll find your heart more sensitized to His voice. You'll better understand His heart and the things He likes to do and say, which will make it easier to discern when He is speaking to you.

Clarifying the Difference

Belief can happen by simply agreeing intellectually to a piece of information—even if that information is imagined. Belief does not require any sort of actual reality. Billions of people on this planet believe things that aren't true, and none of those beliefs can save them.

All a person has to do to believe something is decide to agree that certain information is true. The source of that information is irrelevant. The only thing that matters is that the information is agreeable.

Faith only happens when we believe God. Sometimes the things God says are not "agreeable." Sometimes He says things that are emotionally uncomfortable to us or that seem illogical. But if we will entrust ourselves to Him, God will prove His word true. That's how faith is grown.

I would even go so far as to call faith "partnership." Faith requires that I entrust myself to a Person. Belief can happen when I'm all alone, but faith is only possible when there's another Person to whom you can entrust yourself.

It's Okay to Recognize Your Lack of Faith

We Christians seem to have a delusional desire to believe that our faith is perfect. It pains us to hear someone suggest that there might be something lacking in our faith.

Jesus regularly rebuked, corrected, and exposed a lack of faith (Matthew 6:30; 8:26; 14:31;

16:8; 17:20; Mark 4:40; 16:14; Luke 8:25; 12:28). But whenever He saw faith, He made a point to commend it—sometimes even marveling at it (Matthew 8:10; 9:22,29; 15:28; Mark 5:34; 10:52; Luke 7:9,50; 8:48; 17:19; 18:42). Interestingly, the people He most often corrected for a lack of faith were His disciples, and the people He most often praised for faith were not. As a matter of fact, you'll be hard pressed to find one place where He praises the twelve for their faith. Is it such a stretch to think that He might correct us for our own lack of faith?

The biggest struggle we tend to have is the assumption that having a lack of faith brings our salvation into question. After all, we are saved "by grace through faith." If we don't have faith, how can we be saved?

What we miss is that it's possible to have faith for one thing and not another. For example, I've already explained to you how fully I trust my wife. But if I'm standing on the roof of my house, and my wife says, "Jump! I'll catch you!" there's no way I'm going to jump! Why? I know my wife's limitations. If I jump, we'll both be injured.

In this case, I'm not trusting my wife. But does this mean that we're not married? Does it mean that I don't have faith in her for other things? Of course not. It simply means that in this one regard, I don't trust her because I know her limitations.

God has no limitations, but sometimes, we perceive them where they don't exist. God says, "Jump! I'll catch you!" and we reply, "I'm not sure if You can," or, "I'm not sure if You really want to." This doesn't bring our salvation into question, and it doesn't mean we don't have faith in God for other things. It simply means that in one particular area, we expect limitations to exist where they do not.

Naturally, I'm not talking about literally jumping off a building (even Jesus knew better than to do that—Luke 4:9-12). But when it comes to healing ministry, we have often chosen to believe information from other sources (teachers, scientists, pastors, authors, friends, and our own imaginations) rather than simply believing God.

If we pretend that our faith is perfect, then when people aren't healed, we'll attribute it to God.

Whenever I encounter people who say "God doesn't always want to heal" and use that as an excuse for why the sick aren't healed through their prayers, I like to ask, "Then why did Jesus heal every single person who came to Him?"

Usually, the answer is something like, "Well, that was Jesus!"

"What makes Him any different?"

"Well," they answer, "He was God."

"So let me get this straight," I reply, "God doesn't want to heal everybody, but Jesus healed everybody because He was God?"

Whether you believe Jesus was God in the flesh (John 1:1-14) or whether you falsely believe He was only a mere human being doing the will of God, you must at least agree that if He healed everyone, then it's because it was always God's will. And if God doesn't change from one generation to the next, then we must conclude that this is still His will.

If we pretend that our faith is perfect, then we won't be the least bit challenged to change when people aren't healed. We'll assume it's God's will and won't seek to grow or become more like Jesus (who healed all). But if we recognize our own lack of faith, then we will humble ourselves before the Lord, submit to the working of His spirit in our lives, and learn to trust Him more completely.

Moving Mountains

Immediately following Jesus' words of correction about the lack of faith that kept His disciples from setting the epileptic boy free, He said, "Truly I tell you, if you have faith as small as a mustard seed, you can say to this mountain, 'Move from here to there,' and it will move. Nothing will be impossible for you." (Matthew 17:20). Soon after this, Jesus cursed a fig tree, and it quickly withered. He used that teachable moment to remind His disciples to have faith: "Truly I tell you, if you have faith and do not doubt, not only can you do what was done to the fig tree, but also you can say to this mountain, 'Go, throw yourself into the sea,' and it will be done" (Matthew 21:21).

For Jesus, the evidence of faith is that a mountain moves. Interestingly, we don't see many literal mountains flying around the earth. There's a reason for that. It's not because we don't believe it's possible. It's because faith requires hearing, and God doesn't seem to be telling many of us to throw literal mountains around. But He did tell us to heal the sick (Matthew 10:8), and any time God tells us to do something, faith makes that thing possible.

Again, faith is synonymous with partnership—it involves me doing my own part while wholeheartedly trusting God to do His part. Believing in God's power and will to heal isn't enough. I have to actually partner with Him in the moment.

Many times, I have tried to minister healing to someone without seeing results. In those moments, I had all the belief in the world that God wanted it to happen. My understanding of God's nature and His will on the matter were great. But beliefs don't heal people. Faith heals people. Somehow, despite having all the belief in the world, I failed to fully entrust myself to God.

Sometimes this happens because I do more than what He's telling me to do. Sometimes it's because I do less than what He's telling me to do. Sometimes I'm not sure what He's telling me to do, but I rely too heavily on my own feelings or actions and not enough on His power and love. All these things are a lack of faith because all these things are a lack of true partnership in which He — the God of the Universe — has preeminence.

I need to be clear that I see many people healed without having first heard God's voice. I know that healing ministry was commanded 2,000 years ago, so I don't need a new command. In these cases, I simply rely on the default principles of healing ministry (see Appendix B).

But many times, while already engaged in the process of carrying out these default principles, the Holy Spirit will nudge my heart or whisper into my thoughts. Whenever this happens, it's His way of giving me an opportunity to move into faith (since faith comes from hearing Him). It's an invitation into a partnership that happens on His terms. And if I obey, I know it will happen.

Again, many are healed without these subtle instructions from the Lord, but I have seen many left unhealed because I ignored these instructions.

Mountains move when we have faith. The

only kind of belief that brings healing is the belief that moves us into faith.

Retrain Your Language

We need to separate out the two terms of *faith* and *belief*. This is the only way that we can eliminate the confusion that presently exists in the Church today.

If you prayed for someone who wasn't healed, don't say that you had faith for it. You had belief for it, but you did not partner with God to bring healing. If you had, then the person would be healed. The "mountain" would have moved.

Many of us *believe* James 5:15, which says that the prayer of *faith* will save the sick. But it's not belief in James 5:15 that heals people; it's faith that heals people! The word "will" is important. Scripture here promises that when faith is present, the person "will" be healed. But where doctrine is perfect and where beliefs are certain, people are only healed when these things translate into partnership with the God who heals.

So if you pray for a sick person who isn't healed, don't call it the "prayer of faith." It was a prayer of belief, but partnership with God did not occur. And never complain about a lack of healing saying, "I don't understand why it didn't happen! I had so much faith!" If that were true, then the person would be healed. Instead, you had certainty in your heart, and you had solid belief, but you still did not manage to partner with God in that moment, and that's faith.

Faith Grows

As mentioned in Appendix A, Paul wrote to the Thessalonian Christians saying that he thanked God "because your faith is growing more and more" (2 Thessalonians 1:3).

Hebrews 12:2 calls Jesus the "Author and Perfecter of faith." Jesus gives you your faith, and He perfects your faith.

In Romans 12:6, Paul instructs the believers that, "If your gift is prophesying, then prophesy in proportion to your faith." A few verses earlier, he instructed, "...think of yourself with sober judgment, in accordance with the faith God has distributed to each of you" (Romans 12:3).

Now consider those verses in light of your understanding of faith as partnership. Paul thanked God that the Thessalonians were growing in their partnership with God. Jesus is the One who gives us a measure of trust in this relationship, and He is also the One who grows that trust and strengthens our faith in the One who is trustworthy. If we minister prophetically, then we should only say those things that are said in partnership with God. And we should only think of ourselves in light of that which God has spoken to be true about us.

Allow Jesus to grow your faith through the working of the Holy Spirit in your life. Learn to trust God more than you do today. Learn to hear His voice and partner with Him in humility. As you do these things, I guarantee that you'll see the number of healings and miracles in your ministry increase in frequency.

APPENDIX D:

The Difference Between Gifts of Healing & Healing Ministry

Art Thomas

One of the common objections I hear regarding my conviction that God wants to use all believers to minister healing comes from two passages in First Corinthians 12.

> **1 Corinthians 12:7-11** — Now to each one the manifestation of the Spirit is given for the common good. To one there is given through the Spirit a message of wisdom, to another a message of knowledge by means of the same Spirit, to another faith by the same Spirit, *to another gifts of healing* by that one Spirit,

to another miraculous powers, to another prophecy, to another distinguishing between spirits, to another speaking in different kinds of tongues, and to still another the interpretation of tongues. All these are the work of one and the same Spirit, and he distributes them to each one, just as he determines. (NIV, emphasis added)

1 Corinthians 12:27-31 — Now you are the body of Christ, and each one of you is a part of it. And God has placed in the church first of all apostles, second prophets, third teachers, then miracles, then gifts of healing, of helping, of guidance, and of different kinds of tongues. Are all apostles? Are all prophets? Are all teachers? Do all work miracles? *Do all have gifts of healing?* Do all speak in tongues? Do all interpret? Now eagerly desire the greater gifts. (NIV, emphasis added)

The implication of these two passages seems at first glance to state that healing is only to be practiced by some and not all.

For many years, this is what I too believed and taught. And it was even observable—I knew people who had gifts of healing. And I also knew that I wasn't seeing anyone healed, so I clearly had a different gift. That seemed to settle it—that is, until I started thinking critically about it.

Gifts of Healing and God's Will

The way I used to believe seemed to treat gifts of healing like a magic power that was somehow more powerful than the will of God. None of us would ever outright say such a thing, but follow the logic: We say that if a person isn't healed when we pray, the reason is because it wasn't God's will. But then, if someone with a gift of healing comes along, the person we couldn't heal is now healed, and we're required to either believe that God wanted to use that person and not anyone else, or that the person had a gift that trumped God's will.

Gifts of healing do not trump the will of God; they illustrate it.

Let's think about this again. If I pray for a person who isn't healed, but then someone with a gift of healing prays and the person is healed, I must conclude that God's will was for the person to be healed. And that puts me in a serious pickle when I realize that God wanted to heal the person but my own prayers were ineffective. Either God didn't want to use me and did want to use the person with the gift, or God wanted to heal the person all along, but the gift is what accomplished His will. Either way, I can no longer use the excuse that it wasn't God's will.

Gifts of healing prove the will of God and accomplish His desire to heal. A similar principle applies to every spiritual gift.

Defining Spiritual Gifts

Before we can clarify the difference between gifts of healing and the ministry of healing, we need a working definition of spiritual gifts.

We know from First Corinthians 12 that they are given by the Holy Spirit to human beings. Jesus explained how the Holy Spirit gives things to us when He taught in John 16:13-15 that "when He, the Spirit of truth, comes, He will guide you into all the truth. He will not speak on His own; He will speak only what He hears, and He will tell you what is yet to come. He will glorify Me because it is from Me that He will receive what He will make known to you. All that belongs to the Father is Mine. That is why I said the Spirit will receive from Me what He will make known to you."

Jesus described how the Holy Spirit operates. The Holy Spirit receives something from Jesus (which ultimately belongs to the Father) and makes that thing known to us. Every good and perfect gift ultimately comes from the Father (James 1:17), but everything that belongs to the Father also belongs to Jesus. In fact, as you'll see in a moment, these spiritual gifts are actually expressions of Jesus Himself.

When Paul talks about these gifts, which the Holy Spirit distributes, he always couples the teaching with words about us being the Body of Christ, each expressing different parts of Jesus (Romans 12:3-8 and 1 Corinthians 12). That's because when we demonstrate spiritual gifts, we are expressing pieces of Jesus. The Holy Spirit has taken those pieces of Jesus and distributed them to us by grace (that's what the word "gift" means). And when we express them in ministry, we are "faithfully administering God's grace in its various forms" (1 Peter 4:10, NIV84).

Romans 12:6-8 lists gifts such as encouragement and giving. Would it be right to say that God has only called some people to encourage others? Would it be right to say that only certain people with special gifts are supposed to give generously? Similarly, First Corinthians 12:9 mentions a gift of faith. Are we to believe that only a few people who find favor with God can actually have faith?

Obviously, there's a difference between gifts (demonstrated by specific individuals according to the wise distribution of the Holy Spirit) and the things that are expected of every believer.

My conclusion is that gifts are Holy-Spirit-given pieces of Jesus that reveal Him in His fullness. While I might personally encourage you and make you feel good, someone else might encourage you so deeply that you feel like Jesus Himself just spoke into your life. That's a gift. The Holy Spirit took Jesus' encouragement and distributed it to a person who then faithfully administered it to you. Similarly, while one person's natural hospitality might be a nice blessing, another person's hospitality might be a direct expression of the hospitality of Jesus, touching lives more deeply than mere human effort could accomplish. And while every Christian has a measure of faith (and couldn't be a Christian apart from it), sometimes the Holy Spirit takes Jesus' faith and distributes it to a person for a specific task. And who has more faith than the risen, glorified Son of God who physically sits at the right hand of the Father in heaven and looks Him in the eye? Now that's faith! And that's a gift that only happens by grace.

In each of these cases, the difference between spiritual gifts and normal ministry is that normal ministry is based on our personal growth in the Lord while gifts often transcend our current growth and allow us to express some aspect of Jesus in a way beyond our current ability — a way that directly reveals Jesus.

The Greek word for "gift" is directly related to the Greek word for "grace." Gifts are things we have not grown into or earned. Rather, they are given to us through the unmerited, unwarranted, undeserved favor of God. Naturally, the "ordinary" ministry we all walk in is also an expression of grace; the difference is that some expressions of grace are limited by our current growth in Christ while other expressions of grace transcend our current growth in Christ. These are the gifts.

One of the clearest ways to identify that a person is operating in a spiritual gift is when you see powerful ministry taking place, and yet the person is unable to articulate how or why that ministry works (and how or why it could work in another person's life). In other words, they are unable to train others to do the same things. Sometimes, they may seem confused as to why others don't simply do what they do. It seems so natural to them that they can't comprehend a person functioning any differently. This has even given rise to wrong teachings in the Church as people with gifts try to explain why they can do something that others can't.

Gifts of Healing

And this brings us to gifts of healing. Just as there's a difference between the service expected of every Christian and the service demonstrated by those with a "gift of service," there is a difference between the ministry of healing that's available to every believer and the "gifts of healing" described in the Bible.

First, notice that it says "gifts of healing" in First Corinthians 12:9. The term is plural. In fact, the New King James Version renders it "gifts of healings." This is the only item in the list that is presented in a plural form. Apparently, there is more than one gift of healing.

To be honest, I can't offer you a biblical answer for why this is or what Paul meant. However, based purely upon observation, I have a hunch. There was a time before my wife and I were involved in healing ministry when every person she prayed for with a degenerative eye disease was healed. She couldn't explain how or why — we didn't even really understand healing theology at the time — but it happened consistently for a period of time. Similarly, I know a man who, for a time, saw every wrist or hand problem he prayed for completely healed. I would suggest that these people each had a gift of healing — something not based on their understanding of God or their faith per se (or else they could have seen other conditions healed too) but that still produced 100% results within a limited context.

This seems to better fit our definition. Jesus healed every single person who came to Him, so it stands to reason that if the Holy Spirit took some of His healing virtue and distributed it to a believer, the same results would be seen. And since there are gifts (plural), it isn't strange that one person would see 100% results in one thing while another person would see it in another. Plus, in both cases, the person's ministry wasn't based on them having perfect faith or even solid belief. They couldn't even explain to you how it worked. It was simply a gift that was granted by grace.

Gifts of healing—like any other spiritual gift—are glimpses of Jesus in His fullness, intended to reveal to the rest of us what is possible.

For the Common Good

Paul said that spiritual gifts are "given for the common good." (1 Corinthians 12:7). The New King James Version says they are given "for the profit of all."

In each case, the implication is that everyone else in the Church benefits from the gifts. This makes plenty of sense until you observe how the ministries of Jesus and His disciples in the book of Acts appear to use such things as healing, miracles, service, and generosity in the context of evangelism and street ministry far more often than in synagogue or church meetings. In other words, gifts aren't trapped inside the church context—they're for ministry to the world too. How, then, does the entire Church benefit from the operation of spiritual gifts?

Think with me again: Spiritual gifts are glimpses of Jesus. They are the means by which the Holy Spirit makes Jesus known in His fullness through the entire Body of Christ. When every Christian operates in spiritual gifts, we see a clear picture of Jesus in action because these gifts are pieces of Him. The Holy Spirit brought those things to us from Jesus and then distributed them to each one just as He determined.

When I saw my wife ministering healing to degenerative eye diseases with 100% success, I had to come to terms with the fact that God actually wanted every single degenerative eye disease healed. Thus, I benefitted from her gift. When I see a Christian serve in a way that reveals the self-sacrifice of Jesus, it inspires me to serve with the same intensity, reminding me what is possible. When I see a gift of leadership, I'm taught what it looks like when Jesus leads people, and I am sharpened in my own leadership skills. When I see a gift of faith, I am challenged to trust God more than I already do. And when I see a gift of generosity, I discover how stingy I am and how much more I could be giving.

In all these ways, spiritual gifts reveal what is possible in Christ, and we all benefit from seeing Him in action. The old way of thinking about spiritual gifts tends to exempt us from doing much for God—we look at someone doing something amazing, and we say, "Wow, they must have a gift!" Viewing gifts as revelations of Jesus, though, challenges all of us to become more like Him as we discover just how much His grace has made possible. Spiritual gifts are for the common good!

Every Believer's Ministry

When Paul asked the question, "Do all prophesy?" he was not saying that not everyone *can* prophesy. And when he asked, "Do all speak in tongues?" he was not saying that not everyone *can* speak in tongues.

Only two chapters later, Paul talks about what will happen if an unbeliever walked in while everyone was speaking in tongues or while everyone was prophesying (1 Corinthians 14:23-25). And in verse 31, he says that, "you can all prophesy in turn so that everyone may be instructed and encouraged."

The question, "Do all prophesy?" is like asking, "Do all wear blue shirts?" No. Of course not. But *can* all wear blue shirts? *Can* all prophesy?

Prophecy — in its simplest form — is nothing more than hearing from God for someone else and then speaking it to them. Can't we all hear God's voice? Jesus said, "My sheep hear My voice" (John 10:27). In fact, He said that no one comes to Him without having first heard God's voice (John 6:44-45). There's no such thing as a Christian who can't hear God. Is it that much of a stretch to believe that any one of us can prophesy?

How about speaking in tongues? Regardless of your persuasion about speaking in tongues today, one cannot argue with the fact that God's prototype church — the 120 gathered on the day of Pentecost — involved 100% of the people speaking in tongues (Acts 2:4). If Paul had asked that question on the day of Pentecost, the resounding answer would have been, "YES!"

Jesus listed signs that would accompany "those who believe." He said, "In My name they will drive out demons; they will speak in new tongues; they will pick up snakes with their hands; and when they drink deadly poison, it will not hurt them at all; they will place their hands on sick people, and they will get well."

Is "casting out demons" the responsibility of only a few? Or is it the responsibility of all of us? If it's for only a few, why did Jesus correct John for stopping someone from casting out demons in Jesus' name who wasn't one of the disciples (Luke 9:49-50)? Is the promise of divine protection (whether from poison or serpents) a spiritual gift or a promise to all who believe? How about laying hands on the sick and seeing them healed?

In John 14:12, Jesus said, "Very truly I tell you, whoever believes in Me will do the works I have been doing, and they will do even greater things than these, because I am going to the Father." Jesus said "whoever believes in Me" — not "some who believe in Me." And He said we "will do even greater" — not "will do only a fraction." If you can see it in Jesus' ministry, then it belongs in your ministry.

There are gifts, which are fuller expressions of Jesus that stretch the faith of the Church, and there are signs, which accompany every believer as we grow in our faith in Jesus. Both are necessary. Without signs, the working of the Spirit through the Church becomes sporadic at best. And without gifts, the Church never sees the fullness of what's possible.

If there's one thing to take away from this teaching, it's simply this: Do not limit God with excuses such as "that's not my gift." Even if you disagree with my conclusion about the difference between gifts and signs, I'm sure you can at least agree that it's the Holy Spirit who decides what gift you receive — not you. Never limit God by assuming that He won't use you in a particular way. And like Paul instructed the Corinthians: eagerly desire spiritual gifts (1 Corinthians 14:1).

APPENDIX E:

Causes of Sickness

Art Thomas

First John 3:8 says that the reason Jesus came into the world was to destroy the devil's work. Since He healed everyone who came to Him, many have assumed that every sickness and disease is the direct result of a demonic presence; but this is not true. Demons can indeed cause diseases and sickness — and they often do — but they are only one possible culprit in a long list.

The first work of the devil that we read about in Scripture is the tempting of Adam and Eve, which led to the fall of humankind. With this fall, death and disease came into the world — things unimaginable in the Garden of Eden. So ultimately, all sickness is rooted in the work of the devil and the sin of mankind. But this can lead to another misconception: that if a Christian is sick, then there must be sin in his or her life that is causing it.

The purpose of this list is not to say that one must determine the cause of a sickness before it can be healed—that is simply not true. Rather, it is to discourage a practice that has been prevalent in the Church throughout the past few decades: Blaming the victim.

Many people with chronic illnesses—specifically Christians—have been told that there must be some hidden sin in their life causing their condition. These faithful saints have often spent years begging God to tell them what their secret sin is, repenting over and over in hopes of earning some relief. Thus, the well-meaning believers who were trying to troubleshoot their friend's condition (without taking personal responsibility for their own lack of faith) actually did more harm than good—piling condemnation like a Pharisee onto an already struggling person.

There is no need to memorize the following list because the source of the problem is really irrelevant when you're ministering healing. Jesus never stopped to figure out the cause. In fact, when the disciples wanted to know the cause of a man's blindness, Jesus shrugged it off as irrelevant and proceeded to heal him (John 9:1-3). Simply read this list to help establish the fact that sicknesses have many different causes, but they all have the same solution: Minister the healing power and authority of Jesus Christ with genuine faith in Him.

Environmental

Some sickness happens because our bodies are

sensitive to certain chemicals, organisms, radiation, and other such environmental factors. If your home has black mold in it, for instance, you may develop a related sickness in your lungs. Certain gasses, like carbon-monoxide, can cause physical symptoms of sickness when breathed for any length of time. Some people who have worked with certain technology in the past have developed cancer as a result of prolonged exposure to the radiation. Others have developed lung cancer from second-hand smoke. In all these cases, the reason the person became sick is simply the proximity of something in their physical environment that was detrimental to their body. Being healed from such exposure happens just like any other condition is healed, but it is wise to also deal with the environmental issue so that the problem does not recur.

Heredity

Doctors often ask about the medical history of your family because certain conditions are known to occasionally be passed genetically from one generation to the next. Heart disease, kidney stones, eye problems, allergies, back issues, diabetes, and more can all stem from family history. One of the things that we like to see is physical healing that runs so deeply that it ends the disease for all future generations.

Birth Defects

Some conditions that exist from birth have nothing to do with genetics but may be caused by other situations. Some of these things could have been avoided (like fetal alcohol syndrome) while others are simply random. Whatever the cause of a birth defect, the real root is that we live in a fallen world, bringing the reason for the condition back to the fall of man and the work of the devil. Jesus destroyed the works of the devil, and even birth defects fit that category.

Injuries

This should be an obvious one: a broken leg is a broken leg. Some conditions are simply the result of physical trauma of some kind. Occasionally, problems from an injury don't surface until much later. For example, I had degenerative disc disease for four years (before God healed me miraculously), but it was believed to have stemmed from an injury I had experienced about ten years before I started seeing symptoms.

Aging

Human beings age — it's a fact of life. Moses managed to age very well: "Moses was a hundred and twenty years old when he died, yet his eyes were not weak nor his strength gone" (Deuteronomy 34:7). Nevertheless, years of hard work (or lack thereof) can take a toll on the human body, which generally degrades over time. Thankfully, the same God who "forgives all your sins and heals all your diseases" also "satisfies your desires with good things so that your youth is renewed like the eagle's" (Psalm 103:3 and 5). Jesus' blood paid for the elderly too!

Self-Care

Poor hygiene, diet, sleep habits, or other lifestyle choices can produce sicknesses and physical problems over time. Years of smoking can produce lung cancer while alcohol abuse can result in liver failure. Prolonged sun exposure can cause sunburn, but allowing it to happen again and again can result in skin cancer. Similarly, many dental and oral problems can be avoided by simply brushing your teeth and flossing. Amazingly, our experience has been that none of these things exempt a person from being healed. Once the person is healed, though, we like to encourage them in proper self-care to avoid similar problems in the future.

Curses

During my travels in Africa, I have met many people whose Christian testimony was that a witchdoctor had cursed them, causing a sickness, disease, or mental illness; but then a Christian came and ministered healing or deliverance in Jesus' name. And once they were free and saw the power of God, they chose to give their lives to Jesus. There is also a

Christian side to this, like when Paul cursed the sorcerer Elymas with blindness "for a time" (Acts 13:10-11). All curses are reversible because the name of Jesus has supreme authority.

Emotional Compromise

Doctors have found that certain negative emotions (like anger, bitterness, fear, self-hatred, or anxiety) can cause biochemical secretions and nervous reactions in the body that produce illness over time. For example, IBS and heart palpitations have been linked to long-term anxiety. Similarly, migraine headaches, TMJ, and chronic back pain are sometimes linked to repressed anger. These sicknesses are purely the natural physical outcomes of prolonged exposure to normal physiological expressions of emotion. We have seen many cases where these conditions are healed through laying hands or speaking with authority in Jesus' name, but if the underlying emotion is not surrendered to the cross, the person may find himself or herself back in the same condition as before.

Psychosomatic

Similar to emotional compromise, doctors have found that people can think themselves into an illness. The human mind can cause such symptoms as tremors, nausea, chest pain, headaches, fast breathing. None of these are an actual illness on their own, but the Lord does offer a solution: The Spirit He has given us produces a sound mind (2 Timothy 1:7).

Side Effects

While it's no laughing matter, I've heard elderly people joke about taking one medication to treat the side effects of another medication, which they are taking to treat the side-effects of another medication! Some conditions are brought on by the very medicine that is supposed to be helping a person. Thankfully, the woman with the issue of blood who had "suffered a great deal under the care of many doctors" was still healed by the power of God (Mark 5:26). For those who have not been healed and must take a medication (but are afraid of possible side effects), it is encouraging to remember that Jesus said "those who believe" would be unharmed by deadly poison (Mark 16:18).

Sin (Direct Correlation)

Some conditions are directly connected to sin. Perhaps the easiest to recognize would be sexually transmitted diseases, which are extremely rare among heterosexual couples who are monogamous and remained celibate prior to marriage. If a person is having sex outside of such a Biblically-sanctioned union and contracts an STD, one could argue that they deserve their situation. But Jesus took the penalty for our sin and paid the price for our complete wholeness.

Sin (Indirect Correlation)

The spiritual law of sowing and reaping has been known to produce physical problems in response to sin. For example, I know a woman who was healed of ovarian cancer after she repented of the bitterness she held in her heart against her mother and sister. The sowing and reaping connection was almost eerie: her bitterness against two prominent women in her life had led to her own womanhood being attacked. I have seen many similar cases. The danger of this teaching, though, is that we may start to search for sinful roots behind every condition we encounter; or we may begin to believe that the person cannot be healed until their sin is exposed. But Jesus never fished for sinful roots and simply healed every person through physical contact or authority. James 5:15 teaches us that when a person is healed, any sin in their life is automatically forgiven.

Evil Spirits

Finally, some sicknesses and diseases are caused by evil spirits. Jesus cast out a deaf and mute spirit, a spirit of epilepsy, and a spirit of infirmity that had caused a crippling back condition (among many others). Not every sickness or disease is directly caused by the presence of a demon, but not every sickness or disease is purely medical. Even conditions that can be observed and diagnosed medically may be the work of a demon. See Appendix F for more information.

APPENDIX F:

Healing Ministry and Demons

Art Thomas

As mentioned in Appendix E, demons are only one of many causes of illness. And while the principle of casting out demons during healing ministry was covered in Appendix B, it seemed like a good idea to offer a little more insight into the operation of demons in relation to healing ministry.

Please understand that I have no interest at all in giving attention to evil spirits. Writing about demons is not anti-Christian — if it were, then many of the Bible's authors would have been in sin. Even Jesus taught His disciples about demons.

Paul said that we are not unaware of the devil's schemes (2 Corinthians 2:11). Accordingly, it is actually appropriate for the Church to be aware of how the enemy works—not to become fixated or enthralled with the kingdom of darkness, but to remove the cloak of mystery that has allowed the devil to intimidate too many believers.

Everything presented in this section is for the purpose of helping you to rise above the assault of the enemy and see the victory of Jesus as you minister healing.

How Spirits Affect Physical Bodies

Your physical body is designed by God to respond to the spiritual realm. If it didn't, you wouldn't be alive. James said that a human body without a spirit is dead (James 2:26). At creation, God formed man's body from the dust of the ground, but he didn't come to life until God also breathed into him a spirit (Genesis 2:7).

How many times have you sensed the presence of God in a church service or felt your hair stand on end in the presence of evil (like in Job 4:15)? The fact is, your body reacts to the spiritual realm. In fact, the writer of Hebrews shows that there are those who "by reason of use have their senses exercised to discern both good and evil" (Hebrews 5:14, NKJV). The Greek word here for "senses" literally means your physical perception. So it is possible over time to learn to discern things in the spiritual realm based on what you feel in your physical body (just like when you physiologically feel the presence of God in a place and are able to recognize that it's Him).

When God puts a human spirit in a body, we come to life. But our bodies often respond to other spiritual influences as well. When the Holy Spirit touches a human body, we often see physical results. Some people are healed or set free from addictions. Some people shake. Some people weep. Some people laugh. It therefore is no stretch to see that an evil spirit can affect a person's physical body as well.

Some like to think that demons can only influence our emotions. If you ask a scientist to explain what emotions are, he or she will tell you that emotions are simply biological secretions of chemicals from glands within our bodies. If the Holy Spirit can produce joy or peace (presumably by producing the right mix of chemicals in your human body), is it strange to think that a demon could cause a gland in someone's body to secrete an imbalance of a particular chemical?

The fact is, demons can affect human bodies. In Luke 13:11, "a woman was there who had been crippled by a spirit for eighteen years. She was bent over and could not straighten up at all." When the demon was cast out, verse 13 says that "immediately she straightened up and praised God." I'm not sure what this demon was doing specifically—perhaps causing certain nerves to be inflamed, bringing weakness to discs in the spine, or maybe even something else. But I do know that as soon as the demon left, her physical health was restored in a dramatic way!

Demons caused sickness throughout Scripture. They could make people unable to speak (Matthew 9:32-33; 12:22; Mark 9:17-18,24-25), see (Matthew 12:22), and hear (Mark 9:17-18,20,25). They were known to cause seizures (Mark 1:26; 9:17-18,20,22,25; Matthew 17:15,18; Luke 9:39), sores on the skin (Job 2:7), and boils and other bodily afflictions (Psalm 78:49). Satan can directly cause illness (Job 2:7-8) and even death (Job 1:19).

Addressing Demons in Healing Ministry

As mentioned in Appendix B, any time pain moves or intensifies during healing ministry, a demon is clearly at work. Knowing what you now know about demons causing problems in physical bodies, do you see how a demon moving would cause a person's pain to move? And do you see how an aggravated demon trying to intimidate us from casting him out might amp up the pain being afflicted on the person?

The way to cast out a demon is simply to tell it to leave in Jesus' name. I find it unfortunate that we've taken one isolated case (the Geresene demoniac in Mark 5:1-20) and made it a model for healing ministry. I believe this story is only recorded because it stood out among all the others and made it memorable. The most common form of deliverance ministry practiced by Jesus was much less dramatic:

> **Matthew 8:16** — When evening came, many who were demon-possessed were brought to him, and he drove out the spirits with a word and healed all the sick. (NIV)

Jesus did it with a single word. I don't know what that word was (and it's probably just as well because we might make a formula out of it), but the fact is that He didn't have a long, drawn-out conversation with demons. He didn't have to find out their name or anything like that. He simply told them to get out.

In Mark 5:8, we have the only account of a demon not leaving the first time Jesus commanded it to do so. Again, this was the exception rather than the rule. But it encourages us in the event that a demon is commanded to leave and nothing happens.

In most cases, I have found that deliverance ministry is not the least bit dramatic. Often, the person simply feels peace without anything strange happening. Sometimes the pain simply stops. The most common experience is that the demon leaves so quickly and effortlessly, I'm sometimes left wondering for a while if there actually was any demon at all.

In other cases, demons are more vocal or demonstrative. I once chased a woman from an African village around a field commanding the demon to leave as she galloped on all four limbs like a wild animal. She finally screamed, collapsed, and was set in her right mind. These are the stories we like to tell, but they're not the norm.

In fact, any time a demon tries speaking through a person, I command it to be quiet. There is nothing the demon has to say that I want to hear, and I don't believe it's right to allow them to make a puppet out of the person. Deliverance ministry is not ministry to demons — it's ministry to people. Focus on the person, not the spirit afflicting them.

If a spirit won't leave, there are two possible reasons: (1) it's being stubborn, like the one Jesus encountered in Mark 5:8, or (2) I lack faith (see Appendix C). If I have faith like Jesus, then even the stubborn ones will leave.

And this gives us an indicator of how we are to persevere. The only way the demon will leave is if you remain in faith, and faith involves being more impressed with Jesus than you are with a demon. Do not allow the enemy to frustrate you, intimidate you, worry you, or cause you to fear. If you start to feel any of these feelings, take them to Jesus and surrender them to Him. Let Him give you faith and peace in return.

A Word about Prayer and Fasting

Some might suggest that there's a third possible reason why a demon might not leave. Jesus once said, "This kind can come out only by prayer," and some manuscripts add "and fasting" (Mark 9:29).

Interestingly, the way many Christians respond to this verse is completely contrary to the way Jesus handled the situation. "When Jesus saw that a crowd was running to the scene, He rebuked the impure spirit. 'You deaf and mute spirit,' He said, "I command you, come out of him and never enter him again."'" (Mark 9:25). Notice that Jesus didn't pray, and He certainly didn't leave the boy for a few days while He fasted. Jesus simply commanded the spirit to leave.

In other words, Jesus wasn't prescribing a method of deliverance. He was pointing to a lifestyle of prayer and fasting that somehow positioned Him to speak with an authority that the disciples couldn't.

There's a reason for this: Prayer and fasting are matters of intimacy with God. When Jesus taught about these topics in Matthew 6:5-18, He put them squarely within the context of intimacy with the Father—doing them not in the eyes of man but in the eyes of the Father alone. "Then your Father, who sees what is done in secret, will reward you." (Matthew

6:6,18).

The word "intimacy" implies that only you and one other person know about something, and that's what Jesus is talking about here.

So when Jesus said, "This kind can come out only by prayer and fasting," He was really pointing out that some demons only come out when we have an abiding relationship with God. And if you recall from Appendix C, this abiding relationship with God is the place where faith happens.

There are three reasons I know Jesus was talking about faith and relationship with God here. First, in Matthew's account of the same story, Jesus says the demon didn't leave because the disciples lacked faith (Matthew 17:20). Either one of the Gospel writers is wrong, or they're both referring to the same thing. Second, Jesus said there would be people who cast out demons but never knew Him (Matthew 7:22-23). And third, we have an example in Acts 19:13-16 of people who were driving out demons "in the name of Jesus whom Paul preaches," not really having any sort of first-hand relationship with Jesus. The passage shows that this method was working until seven guys tried it with a demon who apparently only comes out through relationship with God. That spirit answered them, "'Jesus I know, and Paul I know about, but who are you?' Then the man who had the evil spirit jumped on them and overpowered them all. He gave them such a beating that they ran out of the house naked and bleeding" (Acts 19:15-16).

Prayer and fasting are not methods of twisting God's arm and convincing Him to do what we want. They are methods of entering intimacy with God and humbling ourselves so that He can exalt us to accomplish what He wants (Luke 1:52; James 4:10; and 1 Peter 5:6). James 4:6 tells us that greater grace and greater favor go to the humble.

When God described fasting through the prophet in Isaiah 58:5-9, He called it not only a humbling of oneself (verse 5) but a humbling of oneself for a purpose: to set the oppressed free, produce an experience of His Kingdom on earth (by feeding the hungry, clothing the naked, and sheltering the poor), and cause one's light to "break forth like the dawn" — in other words, bring people into their true purpose and identity.

When you fast, you humble yourself before the Lord in intimacy. And when you humble yourself before Him, He exalts you. In other words, He lifts you up to a place where you can minister to others with greater authority than you might have seen without having humbled yourself. This isn't earned authority; it's special favor promised to the humble.

Sure, there are other ways of humbling yourself, but fasting is one of the most practical ways to purposefully value the spiritual realm above the physical for a set period of time while you humbly worship God in intimacy.

Some demons only leave because we have intimacy and relationship with God. Prayer and fasting are two ways of cultivating that relationship. And when the relationship is functioning properly — when you're partnering with God in faith — you will see results.

APPENDIX G:

Reasons Symptoms Sometimes Return

Art Thomas

Occasionally I'm asked if I have ever seen a person healed only to have the sickness or disease return to them a short time later. As a matter of fact, I see it fairly often. In my experience, I've noticed three basic reasons:

1) Psychology
2) Unchanged Stimulus
3) Spirit of Infirmity

Psychology

This is something a lot of healing ministers want to

avoid talking about, but if we're going to show integrity in this ministry, then it must be addressed. Sometimes people are so wrapped up in the emotion of the moment that they feel like they're healed. The human brain is powerful and can produce biological painkillers as a person experiences a euphoric state. Thus people sometimes feel better just long enough for us to grab their testimony. The skeptic's accusation of hypnotism is unfortunately occasionally true.

For this reason, I try to put certain safeguards in place. First, I don't try to create an "atmosphere" with a particular kind of music or lighting. When others set these things up, I'll minister in that setting, but I refuse to rely on it or even request it (after all, you won't find such an atmosphere on the street or in a grocery store, so it clearly isn't necessary). Second, I try not to create hyped-up scenarios for healing. If I'm ministering healing in front of a group of people, I'll be very careful to remain down-to-earth, soft-spoken, and relational. Third, I try not to use many words and move very quickly. This keeps the skeptic from accusing me of manipulating the person's emotions with verbal patter. And fourth, I avoid sudden shouting, smacking, shoving, or anything like that. These things are completely unnecessary and only serve to support an accusation of hypnotism.

One last thing I often do is follow up with a person—usually about a half hour later. In my experience, if something was psychology, it will have worn off by then, and the person will be of more sober mind to allow further ministry without falling victim to the same emotionalism. Whenever I can check up after longer periods (sometimes days, months, or even a year later), I'll do so.

Unchanged Stimulus

If I whack my hand with a hammer, you minister healing to it, and then I smack my hand with a hammer again, then I didn't lose my healing. I just did the same thing to my hand that happened to it in the first place!

If a person has lung cancer and God heals them, the smart thing for that person to do would be to stop smoking, lest the same condition stir up again. If cancer returns, it's not because the person lost their healing. It's because the person didn't stop doing the thing that caused their condition.

Sometimes the stimulus for sickness is emotions or conditions in the environment. As mentioned in Appendix E, these things need to be eliminated from a person's life.

If the sickness is caused by sin (either directly or indirectly), the healed person should take Jesus' advice after He healed the man at the Pool of Bethesda: "See, you are well again. Stop sinning or something worse may happen to you" (John 5:14).

Whatever the case, if a particular activity or situation in a person's life caused their condition, the stimulus should be removed in order for the person to remain free from a second onset of that condition.

Spirit of Infirmity

I have seen and experienced cases where a demon

will come and mimic certain symptoms from a person's previous condition. I've learned that the same devil that will try to convince you that you're not saved will also try to convince you that you're not healed. It's all an attack against the same sacrificial blood of Jesus.

In these scenarios, the right course of action is to command the spirit to leave and immediately try doing something that could not be done previously.

These demonically induced recurrences can happen minutes after a healing (which means you need spiritual discernment about what is or is not psychology) or even years after a person was healed. The devil loves to discourage believers and cause us to doubt the power of Jesus' blood to save. Don't allow him a foothold in your mind. Recognize the attack for what it is, and fight it off with faith-based authority in Jesus' name.

About the Movie:
PAID IN FULL

Imagine what would happen if every Christian was equipped to minister physical healing the way Jesus did. That's God's plan for the Church!

In Acts 5:12 and 16, we learn that the believers all met together in a part of the Temple called Solomon's Colonnade, and every sick and tormented person who came to them was healed. In the ministry of Jesus, everyone who touched His body was healed. (See Matthew 14:35-36; Mark 6:56; Luke 4:40; and Luke 6:18-19.) Now, WE are His Body! (See 1 Corinthians 12:27.)

PAID IN FULL is a film about God's continued desire to heal the sick, the diseased, the infirmed, the disabled, and the injured through ordinary people just like you. Meet more than 30 people who practice Christian healing ministry, and:

- o Witness instant miracles happening in public,
- o Hear testimonies of medically-documented healings, and
- o Learn how you too can minister healing in Jesus' name!

Experience a documentary like none other. Discover more than what is happening throughout the world; JOIN IN!

Order your copy today at:
www.PaidInFullFilm.com